MW01630067

BIRMINGHAM'S BEST BITES

On the Cover:
Top row, left to right: Rogue Tavern Pimento Cheese Sliders: page 97, Little Savannah Cherry Poppins Cocktail: page 9, Highlands Bar and Grill Sliced Tomatoes with Marinated Gulf Crab Meat: page 103.

Bottom row, left to right: Hot and Hot Fish Club Tomato Salad: page 83, Dreamcakes Brown Sugar Pound Cake with Bourbon Caramel Glaze: page 172, Bettola Housemade Ricotta and Charred Tomato Crostini: page 51

Published By:
Advance Central Services Alabama.

Library of Congress Control Number: 2015935814

ISBN 978-1-57571-519-3

To order copies of this book, please contact
    Advance Central Services Alabama
    Carl Bates
    2201 4th Avenue North
    Birmingham, Alabama 35203
    cbates@acsal.com
    205-325-2237

BIRMINGHAM'S BEST BITES

FAVORITE RECIPES FROM RESTAURANTS, BARS, & FOOD TRUCKS AROUND THE MAGIC CITY

Food Network Star Martie Duncan & Chanda Temple • Photographs by Arden Ward Upton

Create. Share. Inspire.
A recipe is more than a combination of ingredients. It's the preamble to the moments we share around the dinner table. For 160 years, we have been honored to help create the meals that bring us together.
We're the good heat.
Alagasco

Contents

BIRMINGHAM
PUBLIC LIBRARY

A portion of the proceeds from *Birmingham's Best Bites* will benefit the Birmingham Public Library.

For more information about the library, its resources and programs, please visit www.bplonline.org.

For more information about the library's Eat Drink Read Write Festival, please visit www.bplonline.org/eatdrinkfest.

Introduction

By Martie Duncan

I'm not sure where I got the inspiration to do a cookbook filled with favorite recipes from around Birmingham, but I do remember where I was when it happened: I was sitting with *Birmingham Best Bites* collaborator Chanda Temple at Chez Fonfon one afternoon, discussing the Birmingham Public Library's annual Eat Drink Read Write Festival. Chanda asked me to host the finale party of the weeklong celebration of food and books in the Magic City. Knowing how important the library is to so many people, I was happy to contribute. As a kid, I spent countless days at Birmingham's East Lake Library and probably read every Nancy Drew mystery or book about horses they had in the place. The books I read about foreign lands inspired the love of travel I still have today.

In the midst of this conversation and over desserts of Chocolate Pots du Créme and Toasted Coconut Pecan Cake, we found ourselves planning a cookbook. My thought was that this book (and potentially subsequent editions) could raise funds to help the library produce more events. I also wanted to help raise awareness within the community of the extensive resources the library has to offer. The library is a place to escape, to work, to learn, to dream, and to achieve goals. It is a place of possibilities.

The Eat Drink Read Write Festival was conceived in 2011 by a group that included librarian Haruyo Miyagawa, food writer Shaun Chavis, and Pardis Stitt, co-owner of Highlands Bar and Grill. It was one of those early meetings that sparked an annual event that has now grown to include many of the city's finest restaurants, food companies, and chefs. It is for that reason that I'd like to dedicate *Birmingham's Best Bites* to Pardis and all of our generous chefs and restaurant owners who provided recipes for the cookbook. Thanks to all of you for your tireless dedication to producing good food, providing excellent service, and for always stepping up to help when you are called upon.

The metropolitan Birmingham area's vibrant restaurant landscape is getting more exciting every day. From five-star stalwarts, neighborhood favorites, food trucks, meat and threes, barbeque joints, breweries, and everything in between, Birmingham has become a food destination to rival any in the region. Move over New Orleans and Atlanta. Folks are now traveling to Birmingham just for our food.

Birmingham restaurants are shining on the national stage, too, gathering praise from the culinary world's highest authority, The James Beard Foundation. The James Beard Foundation is a culinary organization dedicated to excellence in the culinary arts. They present their "Oscars" each year, honoring elite restaurants and chefs who have reached the pinnacle of their profession. Leading the way is Chef Frank Stitt's Highlands Bar and Grill. Since 2009, Highlands has been recognized as one of the top restaurants in the USA by the James Beard Foundation.

When I have guests come to Birmingham, the problem isn't where to take them: It is how to squeeze in all of the choices and dishes I cannot wait for them to taste.

I hope you enjoy *Birmingham's Best Bites* as much as I enjoyed being part of it. Many thanks and all the appreciation in the world to the dedicated team who made the book possible: Chanda Temple, Lisa Mitchell Smith, Arden Ward Upton, Moesia Davis, Anne Cain, Grace McNair Headman, Connie Blalock, Chef Chris Vizzina, and Joyce Pettis. The Birmingham, Alabama, Public Library Archives Department went beyond expectations to make the book bigger, better, and more beautiful than I ever imagined. Many thanks to Beth McKern and Alagasco for their unwavering support and to the Birmingham Public Library Board of Trustees and staff for seeing that this project was filled with so many possibilities.

Wishing you good cooking and good times,

Martie Duncan

Birmingham & The James Beard Awards
Birmingham's Impressive List of Winners, Nominees, & Semifinalists

The James Beard Awards are often referred to as the "Oscars" for the food industry. Presented in May each year by the James Beard Foundation, the awards are voted on by over 600 culinary professionals to honor the year's finest chefs, restaurants, journalists, cookbook authors, and other food professionals in the United States.

Chef Frank Stitt, Pardis Stitt, Highlands Bar & Grill
Nominee, Best Chef South, 1996, 1998, 1999, 2000
Winner, Best Chef in the Southeast, 2001
Nominee, *Cooking from a Chef's Point of View: Frank Stitt's Southern Table: Recipes and Gracious Traditions from Highlands Bar and Grill*, 2005
Nominee, Outstanding Chef, 2008
Nominee, Outstanding Restaurant in America, 2009, 2010, 2011
Winner, Who's Who of Food and Beverage in America, 2011
Finalist, Most Outstanding Restaurant in America, 2009, 2010, 2011, 2012, 2013, 2014, 2015

Pastry Chef Dolester Miles, Highlands Bar & Grill
Semifinalist, Outstanding Pastry Chef, 2014, 2015

Chef Chris Hastings, Hot and Hot Fish Club
Semifinalist, Best Chef South, 2007, 2008, 2010, 2011
Winner, Best Chef South, 2012

The Bright Star
Winner, America's Classics, 2010

Chef James Lewis, Bettola
Semifinalist, Best Chef South, 2012, 2013

Nick Pihakis, Jim 'N Nick's Bar-B-Q Restaurant
Semifinalist, Best Restaurateur, 2012, 2013, 2014, 2015

Chef Chris Newsome, Ollie Irene
Semifinalist, Best New Restaurant, 2012
Semifinalist, Best Chef South, 2015

Original Tutwiler Hotel

Days Gone By

By Chanda Temple

A handful of vintage Birmingham menus, which are part of the millions of artifacts preserved in the archives department of the Birmingham Public Library, shows the long tradition of fine dining and appreciation of good food the city has offered through the years.

Downtown hotels such as the original Tutwiler Hotel, at 20th Street and Fifth Avenue North, had French chefs skilled at serving up French feasts. On October 26, 1921, those chefs combined Southern flair with their French food to create a lavish banquet for President Warren G. Harding. He was in town to celebrate Birmingham's 50th anniversary as a city.

His banquet menu featured the following dishes: Canapé Semi-Centennial; Queen Olives; Alabama Gumbo Creole En Tasse; Sweet Potatoes Kilby; Corn Fritters Jefferson; Salad a la Ramsay; Fried Chicken A La Warren G. Harding; Magic City Biscuits; and Tortoni America, assorted cakes.

Another major meal of note was when American aviator Charles Lindbergh visited Birmingham on October 5, 1927, as part of a world tour. A dinner held at Boutwell Auditorium included Canapé Lindbergh; Celery Hearts America; Queen Olives; Milk-fed Chicken "Paris;" Potatoes Memphis; Salade Spirit of St. Louis; Ice Cream Evangeline; and iced tea, according to a menu from that time period.

Such menus suggest that Birmingham has always been more than burgers and barbecue.

"When people think of early Birmingham, they think of mines and mills and a new raw city. But these menus show that there were people here who were already creating gourmet cuisine," says Jim Baggett, head library archivist.

Photos also tell a story of Birmingham's rich food past. Housed in the library's archives department are thousands of photos of Birmingham restaurants, dating back as early as the 1900s. Many of the restaurants in those photos are now closed. However, memories of the restaurants remain with residents.

Places such as Joy Young American Chinese Restaurant, 412 20th Street North, are where people gathered for business lunches, date nights, and special occasions. It opened in 1919 under a different name and later became Joy Young. It had two previous locations, but the location on 20th Street North

President Harding Outside Tutwiler Hotel, 1921

Joy Young Restaurant

was the one that people came to love, according to Todd Keith's book *Birmingham Then and Now*. The downtown location closed in the early 1970s.

Jo Ellen O'Hara, who spent forty-five of her forty-eight years at *The Birmingham News* as the paper's food editor before retiring in 2008, recalls how she often bought the Mandarin lunch for about .99 cents at Joy Young. Choices included chop suey, chow mein, and egg foo young.

"It was a place where everybody went,'' O'Hara says. "When people would come to [college] football games, they'd meet at the [old] Tutwiler in the lobby and go across the street to Joy Young.'' (In the 1950s, the restaurant's chicken egg foo young was .55 cents.)

To this day, people still talk about its egg rolls and egg foo young. But diehard fans don't have to go far to bite into a food flashback. The website for the Chop Suey Inn on Greensprings Highway in Homewood, Alabama, says they are the only place "you'll find authentic Joy Young recipes.'' That includes the egg rolls and egg foo young.

Housed in a retail center off Greensprings Highway near Publix, the Chop Suey Inn has more customers coming in for carry out than sit-down meals. But the food tastes the same as what Birmingham customer Jo Hollins remembers having at Joy Young. "I love coming here,'' Hollins says. "Today, my husband and I are getting the egg foo young with shrimp and egg rolls.'' "We were exercising at Lakeshore and I said, 'Let's treat ourselves. Let's go to Chop Suey Inn.' ''

Other popular Birmingham restaurants from days gone by include Britling Cafeteria, where diners could find decadent desserts at the front of the cafeteria food line before picking up a meat and vegetables. There was also LaParee, Joe's Steakhouse, Loveman's Tearoom, and Mary Beard's.

"On football weekends, you couldn't get into LaParee. You couldn't get into Joy Young. You couldn't get into any restaurant downtown," O'Hara says. "You have to remember, they weren't fancy. They were just good places to eat. Any place that was pretentious, it didn't last long."

Another restaurant that drew a crowd was Cobb Lane Restaurant, where people dined on Tomato Aspic, Chicken Supreme, homemade yeast rolls, and creamy She-Crab Soup.

Positioned just off a brick alley in Birmingham's Five Points South district and shaded by huge oak trees was Cobb Lane Restaurant. It was known for serving classic Southern food with a side of old-world charm. People went there for bridesmaids' luncheons, birthdays, baby showers, or their last day of work. It was truly a place where good memories were made over good food. Virginia Cobb opened Cobb Lane Restaurant in 1948 with homemade dishes that sparked a tremendous following. It switched owners a few times over the years. When the restaurant closed in 2009, that didn't stop followers from yearning for Cobb's food. To this day, people's eyes still glaze over when discussing Cobb's Chocolate Roulage, says Food Network Star finalist and Birmingham entertainment expert Martie Duncan. The roulage was one of Duncan's favorites.

"I learned to make it many years ago and while I never had Mrs. Cobb's actual recipe, I think this is pretty close," Duncan says. "I even created this version for a challenge when I competed on Food Network Star in 2012." Duncan says she had a hard time convincing the Food Network Star judges that in Birmingham, the name for the dessert is roulage, not roulade, which is what the chocolate rolled dessert is typically called. When she made it on the show, all it took was one bite for the judges to fall in love with her dish, which came with a bourbon cream. "Delicious and well done," one judge told Duncan.

While not the easiest dessert to master, it is so worth the effort, Duncan says. (It was the first dessert Duncan made as a child when she started throwing parties.)

"I make it for my nieces for Christmas Eve. It's a family tradition for my family and for many others in Birmingham as well," she says.

Britling Cafeteria, 1950s

Martie's Chocolate Roulage with Bourbon Cream
Inspired by Cobb Lane Restaurant

Softened, unsalted butter (for greasing baking sheet)
5 egg yolks
1 cup granulated sugar
3 ounces bittersweet chocolate, chopped
3 ounces semi-sweet chocolate, chopped
1 teaspoon vanilla extract
1 tablespoon espresso or strong, black coffee, room temperature
5 egg whites
1 cup cocoa powder
2 cups heavy cream
2 teaspoons confectioners' sugar
½ cup bourbon (optional)
Seeds from ½ vanilla bean
1 teaspoon vanilla

Directions:
Prep Time: 30 minutes
Cook Time: 12 minutes plus 30 minutes cool time and chill 2 hours before serving

Preheat oven to 325°F.

Butter a rimmed jelly roll/baking sheet and line with parchment paper. Butter top of paper, especially the corners. Fit a stand mixer with whisk attachment; beat the egg yolks and sugar on medium speed until fluffy, and the sugar is not gritty, about 10-12 minutes. While the eggs are beating, put chocolate in a bowl and melt over a double boiler. When chocolate is melted, remove from heat; let it cool a bit. Set the bowl in some cool water for a few minutes, if necessary. Incorporate the egg mixture into chocolate by adding a little at a time to temper the mixture, so you don't cook the eggs. Add vanilla extract and espresso.

In a clean mixer bowl, and with whisk attachment, beat the egg whites until stiff peaks form. Incorporate ¼ of egg whites into the chocolate mixture, making sure no white streaks remain. Carefully fold in the remaining whites into the chocolate, taking care not to deflate the whites but making sure not to have any white streaks in the batter.

Spread batter in the prepared pan. Bake at 325°F for 10-12 minutes. Remove from the oven and spread a damp tea towel or several damp paper towels over the top of the cake. Let it sit for 30 minutes.

In a clean bowl, with whisk attachment, whip the cream, confectioners' sugar, bourbon, vanilla bean, and vanilla extract on medium speed until stiff peaks form. (Bourbon is optional.)

Carefully turn the cake out onto clean parchment paper, making sure to have 4-5 inches of excess paper at the end to help you roll the cake. Using a fine sieve or sifter, sprinkle ½ cup of cocoa powder over the top of the cake. Use an offset spatula or butter knife to spread the whipped cream mixture over the top, leaving ¼ inch on each side. Using the edge of the parchment paper, carefully roll the cake creating a jellyroll effect. Tuck and roll as you go, peeling back the paper along the way. Put the rolled cake, seam side down, on a platter; cover with plastic wrap, and chill 2 hours before serving. You might even put the cake in the freezer for an hour before serving so that it is easy to slice. Before serving, dust the whole cake with cocoa powder. Carefully slice the cake with a serrated knife and place on chilled plates. Garnish with a light dusting of cocoa powder and fresh berries.

Yield: 1 Chocolate Roulage, about 6-8 slices

While fine dining may have been dominant in Birmingham's past, so was fast food. A popular place to fuel up on burgers, fries, milkshakes, and ice cream sodas was the Ed Salem's Drive-Ins, founded by University of Alabama All-American football player Ed Salem. The first one was located at 10th Avenue and 26th Street North. It opened in 1953 and closed in 1983.

The aroma of burgers and fries filled the air as customers opened the front door, as did the music from the jukebox, Birmingham resident Chervis Isom recalls. If you didn't order inside, curb hops - women in short skirts on roller skates - rolled out to your car to take your order. "Everything was good. It was a first-class place for its time," Isom recalls.

Football legends such as University of Alabama Coach Paul "Bear'' Bryant and Joe Namath visited Ed Salem's, where French fries covered in gravy and the homemade lemon ice box pie were popular. Salem is now deceased, and all of the Ed Salem's Drive-Ins are closed. But people can still get their fix for the fries with gravy, the lemon ice box pie, and more at Salem's Diner in Homewood, which is run by Salem's son, Wayne Salem.

"If it wasn't for Ed Salem's Drive-In, I wouldn't be able to do what I'm doing today,'' Wayne Salem adds. He says they make the ice box lemon pie from scratch daily at his diner. The special touch to it? The 8-10 freshly squeezed lemons in each pie. "It's more refreshing than a key lime pie,'' he says, adding that they sell 8-10 pies a week.

Ed Salem's Drive-In Lemon Ice Box Pie

8-10 fresh lemons, freshly squeezed
2 (14-ounce) cans of Eagle brand condensed milk
2 eggs
1 (9-ounce) graham cracker pie crust

Directions:
Squeeze the lemons and mix with milk and eggs. Pour mixture into pie crust. Preheat oven to 325°F and bake for 10-12 minutes. Remove and let cool. Top with Reddi-wip®. (They use a homemade whip.)

One of Wayne Salem's dishes that has received national attention is his Philly Cheese Steak Sandwich. When CBS late night show host Craig Ferguson was in Homewood to appear at Hoover, Alabama's Stardome Comedy Club in 2007, he stopped by Salem's Diner and had the Philly Cheese Steak Sandwich. Ferguson raved about it on television.

"This diner in Alabama had the best Philly Cheese Steak I've ever tasted," Ferguson said. "And I include Philadelphia."

Birmingham also became known for its meat-and-three eateries such as the Social Grille in downtown Birmingham and the Ensley Grill in Ensley, a neighborhood of Birmingham. Both are now closed.

"The Ensley Grill was the first meat-and-three I went to as a teenager," says Phyllis Wyne, who attended high school in the Ensley area in the mid-1960s. "It was a family restaurant. It was the place to go on Fridays."

"No matter how rich or how poor you were, you could go," adds Wyne. "Blacks and whites went."

But blacks and whites eating together in public places was not always allowed in Birmingham. Jim Crow laws were created to keep the races separate until Birmingham officials repealed all segregation ordinances in July 1963, according to a 2013 timeline from www.al.com. Before 1963, blacks had to get their food at the rear of a restaurant or order from a different area than whites at many establishments.

Black-owned restaurants such as The Seagull, famous for its fried seafood, and Salter's BBQ, known for serving barbeque covered in sauce on top of white bread, sold delicious meals. But the black community yearned for more, says longtime Birmingham resident Delores C. Burgess.

Recognizing a need to offer dining and lodging alternatives for black people, black Birmingham businessman A.G. Gaston built the A.G. Gaston Motel and Restaurant in 1954 on Fifth Avenue

North. The motel would later play a significant role in the city's 1963 civil rights movement, which eventually brought the Reverend Martin Luther King, Jr. to town to help lead the pursuit of equality and justice for blacks.

The motel and restaurant experienced different phases through the years. When it first opened, the restaurant offered "as good as grandma's" Southern cuisine in a cafeteria, and then hamburgers, milkshakes, and icy Coca-Colas in a diner-style setup. It later evolved into a sit-down restaurant with "Gaston" embossed in gold print on the menus, says Marie A. Sutton, author of the new book *The A.G. Gaston Motel in Birmingham: A Historic Landmark*.

A. G. Gaston Motel Matchbook

In 1963, Gaston recruited a married couple from Arkansas to bring a fine dining experience to the restaurant. The couple, Ernest and Carolyn Gibson, succeeded, offering white tablecloths, music, greeters, and waiters in what would become known as a "supper club." The restaurant served lobster, steak, and more for diners eager for something unlike what blacks had access to in the days of segregation, says Sutton.

"One woman talked about how every Sunday her family would go to the restaurant. It was the only place (blacks) could go for fine dining," Sutton says, adding that whites dined there, too.

Celebrities such as Joan Baez, Ike and Tina Turner, Ray Charles, Johnny Mathis, and Nina Simone visited the restaurant. In 1963, King stayed at the hotel and dined at the restaurant. He had grits and eggs for breakfast and anything from fried chicken to barbecue ribs for dinner, Sutton says.

As segregationists' bombings, including one at the motel in May 1963, punctuated Birmingham's civil rights movement, the Gibsons only stayed in Birmingham for about a year. The restaurant and motel closed in 1982. As the empty building sits next to what is now the Birmingham Civil Rights Institute, people hope to see the location reopen as a museum one day.

"The thing about the A.G. Gaston Motel Restaurant was that even though there were turbulent times on the outside, on the inside blacks, whites, young and old could come together at the table for a good meal," says Sutton. "It wasn't about the color of your skin or politics. It was about coming together for the good of human kind."

Photo Credit:
All historic images are from the Birmingham, Alabama, Public Library Archives Department.

Fun Facts About Historic Birmingham Restaurants

By Chanda Temple

- The Birmingham History Center has more than 30 menus from several of the area's now-closed restaurants. Some of those menus include Cobb Lane, Joy Young, Shanghai Low, the Hotel Hillman, Loveman's Tea Room, La Paree and Mary Beard's says Jerry R. Desmond, executive director of the Birmingham History Center.

- The Shanghai Low restaurant, located at Third Avenue and 17th Street North, offered regular Mandarin dishes. Close to the old Jefferson Hotel, the restaurant was popular in the 1930s and 1940s. A menu from that time period shows that a "Chinese Regular Dinner" was .35 cents and a sirloin steak dinner was $1.05.

- In the 1950s, The Birmingham News said that the Joy Young Restaurant had the best fried chicken in Birmingham. The restaurant was also popular for its egg rolls.

- Mary Beard's, located at 215 ½ 20th Street North, offered light lunches, elevator service, and private parties. A menu from the 1930s and 1940s shows that a ham sandwich was .15 cents. They specialized in homemade breads. Rye bread sold for .5 cents.

- Birmingham was founded in 1871, and it didn't take long for it to boom. The city's first major luxury hotel, the Hotel Hillman at Fourth Avenue and 19th Street North, opened in 1901. Its 1902 menu included such rich foods as leg of lamb with mint sauce, mince pie and pineapple pudding a la Richilleu. The hotel also had a men's clothing store, a jeweler and more. "I have a map in my office from 1885 that shows Birmingham had six hotels, six major churches downtown, 27 saloons and 11 brothels," Desmond says. "It was a wild West town. It was growing so fast. You could leave for a year and come back and not recognize it."

La Paree, located on Fifth Avenue North between 19th and 20th Street North, was a steak and seafood restaurant that opened in the 1940s. It also served kabobs, chicken, spaghetti, and lamb chops. It closed in 2003.

Actual menu from Joy Young's American Chinese Restaurant. Courtesy of the Birmingham History Center.

MANDARIN STYLE

PLAIN CHOP SUEY

Plain Chop Suey with Gravy	.35
Extra Fine Chop Suey	.45
Bean Sprout Chop Suey	.45
White Mushroom Chop Suey	.70
Fresh Shrimp Chop Suey	.55
Spanish Chop Suey	.60
Fine Cut Chop Suey	.55
Chop Suey with Almonds	.70
Finne Cut Chop Suey with Mushrooms	.80
Asparagus Tips Chop Suey	.65

BEEF AND VEAL CHOP SUEY

Veal Chop Suey	.50
Veal Chop Suey with Mushrooms	.75
Veal Chop Suey Fine Cut	.60
Veal Fine Cut with Mushrooms	.85
Beef Chop Suey	.50
Beef Chop Suey with Mushrooms	.75
Special Pepper Steak	.70
Beef Chop Suey with Green Pepper	.55
Beef Chop Suey with Tomatoes	.55

GAME POULTRY—JOY YOUNG SPECIAL

Chicken Chop Suey	.60
Chicken Chop Suey with Mushrooms	.85
Chicken Chop Suey with Almonds	.85
Chicken Fine Cut Chop Suey	.70
White Meat Chicken Chop Suey	.70
Chicken Sub Gum Chop Suey	.75
Chicken Sub Gum with Almonds	$1.00
Chicken Liver Chop Suey	.50

Hot Tea Served with all Chop Suey Rice or B. B.

EGGS MANDARIN STYLE

Eggs Fooyoung with Gravy	.40
Chicken Egg Fooyoung	.55
Chicken Liver Egg Fooyoung	.55
Fresh Shrimp Egg Fooyung	.60
Subgum Egg Fooyung	.60
Eggs Canton Style	.50
Mushroom Egg Fooyung	.65
Roast Pork Chinese Style	.40

Hot Tea Served Rice or B. B.

FRIED RICE, CANTON STYLE

Ham, Bacon or Pork, Fried Rice	.40
Chicken, Fried Rice	.55
Fresh Shrimp, Fried Rice	.55
Subgum, Fried Rice	.65
Plain Boiled Rice .05; with Gravy	.10

Hot Tea Served with this Order Only

SPECIAL CHOW MEIN
LUNCH 40c

CHOP SUEY CHOW MEIN
EGGS FOOYUNG
HONEY MIXED FRUITS
COFFE, TEA or MILK

NOODLES

Yat Ko Mein	.25
Extra Yat Ko Mein	.35
Chicken Yat Ko Mein	.35
Yat Ko Mein with Tomato	.35
Wor Mein	.55
Chicken Wor Mein	.70
Subgum Wor Mein	.85
Chicken Sub Gum Wor Mein	1.00

Hot Tea with this Order Only

CHOW MEIN OR FRIED NOODLES

Chicken Chow Mein	.50
Chicken Chow Mein with White Mush.	.85
Chicken Chow Mein with Black Mush.	.85
Chicken Subgum Chow Mein	.85
Chicken Subgum Chow Mein with Almonds	1.10
Plain Chow Mein	.45
Chow Mein with White Mushrooms	.75
Chow Mein with Almonds	.75
Subgum Chow Mein	.75
Subgum Chow Mein with Almond	1.00
Chop Suey Chow Mein	.50
Beef Chow Mein	.75
Fresh Shrimp Chow Mein	.75

Coffee, Iced Tea or Bread and Butter, 5c a
Hot Tea Served with Chow Mein Orders Only

IMPORTED MANDARIN PRESERVES AND FRUITS

Honey Gumget	.15	Mixed Fruits	.15
Honey Ginger	.15	Li Chee Nuts	.15

IMPORTED FINEST CHINESE TEA

Loung Soey Tea, per pot	.15		
Sue Sien Tea, pot .15		Green Tea, pot	.15
O'Long Tea, pot .15		Wo Hop Tea	.10

SALADS

Chicken Salad	.25
Stuffed Egg with Chicken Salad	.30
Potato Salad	.20
Stuffed Tomato with Chicken	.30
Fresh Assorted Fruit Salad	.25
Grape Fruit Salad	.25
Red Salmon Salad	.25
Fresh Shrimp Salad	.25
Waldorf Salad	.25
Combination Salad	.25
Head Lettuce, French Dressing	.15
Head Lettuce, 1000 Island Dressing	.25
Head Lettuce, Roquefort Dressing	.25
Lettuce and Tomato, French Dressing	.25
Sliced Tomato	.15
Sliced Cucumbers	.10
Asparagus Tip Salad	.25

DESSERTS AND FRUITS

Banana Split	.25c	Pineapple Sundae	.15
Strawberry Ice Cream	.10	Chocolate Sundae	.15
Vanilla Ice Cream	.10	Strawberry Sundae	.15
Strawberry Short Cake	—	Orange Sundae	.15
Sliced Bananas, Cream	.10	Fruit Sundae	.15
Sliced Oranges	.10	Peach Sundae	.15
Sliced Peaches	.10	Grapefruit Sundae	.15
Strawberries, Cream	—	Home Made Pie	.10 & .15
Pie a la Mode	.20	Cake a la Mode	.15

Not Responsible for Hats, Coats or Personal Property

Actual menu from Joy Young's American Chinese Restaurant. Courtesy of the Birmingham History Center.

Actual menu from Top of 21. Courtesy of the Birmingham History Center.

The upscale Top of 21 was a penthouse restaurant, which used to be in the building where Highland Manor on 21st Street South is now located. It was popular for prom dates, marriage proposals, or just a night out on the town. "It wasn't black tie but you did dress up," said Jerry R. Desmond, executive director of the Birmingham History Center. "If you ask lifelong residents of Birmingham in their 60s and 70s, they will remember Top of 21."

This menu from the 1960s and 1970s shows that the roast prime rib of beef special was $4.50. It came with choice of soup, a tossed green salad, choice of salad dressing, Yorkshire Pudding, or Baked Idaho Potato, coffee, tea, and choice of dessert.

Courtesy of the Birmingham, Alabama, Public Library Archives Department.

The Birmingham "Magic City'' street sign at the Terminal Station, seen here in the 1930s, represents a time when many visitors would have traveled to Birmingham by train. The sign was removed in the 1950s due to deterioration. Today, it's an image that people immediately associate with old Birmingham. It's also one of the most requested photos from the Birmingham, Alabama Public Library Archives Department. The station was demolished in 1969.

Birmingham's Best Bites Photography by Arden Ward Upton & Mo Davis

The Collins Bar

Cocktails & Drinks

Ain't That A Peach

Hot and Hot Fish Club · Chef Chris Hastings
James Beard Foundation Award Winner

1½ ounces Cathead Small Batch Mississippi Vodka
1½ ounces Chilton County Peach Reduction
½ ounce fresh orange juice
Dry Prosecco
Orange peel

Chilton County Peach Reduction
3-4 Chilton County peaches, baseball size
¼ cup sugar
6 ounces dry white wine
8 ounces water

Directions:
For the Chilton County Peach Reduction: Remove the flesh of the peaches, discarding the pit. Place peaches in a stainless steel nonreactive saucepan. Add remaining ingredients. Bring to a boil on high heat. When the peach reduction is at a rolling boil, reduce heat to low. Allow to simmer for about 10 minutes. Strain into an ice bath using a colander. Makes enough for 8 cocktails. You can store in the refrigerator for up to a week.

To build the cocktail: Combine vodka, peach reduction, and orange juice in a rocks glass. Add ice. Top off with Prosecco and garnish with orange peel.

Yield: 1 serving

Alabama Honeymoon

The J. Clyde

This Alabama-inspired cocktail features ingredients from around the state: Stills Crossroads Moonshine from Union Springs, Back Forty Truck Stop Honey Brown Ale from Gadsden, Southern Oaks Local Honey from Springville, along with fresh-squeezed lemon juice.

1 ounce Stills Crossroads Moonshine
2 ounces Back Forty Truck Stop Honey Brown Ale
¾ tablespoon Southern Oaks Local Honey
½ ounce fresh-squeezed lemon juice
Lemon wedge for garnish
9 ounces crushed ice

Directions:
In a mixing glass, add honey and lemon juice and stir well.

Add moonshine and 9 ounces of ice to mixing glass; shake it.

Pour mixture into a rocks glass, top with the Back Forty Truck Stop Honey Brown Ale, and garnish with a lemon wedge.

Yield: 1 serving

Blood Orange Mojito
Bellinis Ristorante

Simple Syrup
1 cup water
1 cup granulated sugar

Blood Orange Puree
4 blood oranges
1 teaspoon simple syrup
1 teaspoon fresh lemon juice

6-8 whole, fresh mint leaves
½ ounce simple syrup, divided
1¼ ounces Bacardi Limón rum
2 ounces blood orange puree
Juice of ¼ lime
Club soda or Sprite
Mint sprigs (garnish)

Directions:
Prepare Simple Syrup: Combine equal parts granulated sugar and cool water into a pan. Bring to boil over medium heat. Stir to dissolve the sugar. Remove from heat. Allow to cool completely. Pour into a glass jar. (Will keep for 2-3 weeks in the refrigerator.)

Prepare Blood Orange Puree: Segment, peel, and seed oranges. Combine oranges with simple syrup and fresh lemon juice. Purée in a blender or food processor until smooth. Adjust sugar to taste. Makes about ¾ cup.

For the cocktail: Tear 6-8 mint leaves into quarters and drop into a martini shaker. Add ¼ ounce simple syrup. With a muddler, press and twist mint leaves in order to release oils and flavors. Add remaining ¼ ounce simple syrup, and let sit for 30 seconds. Fill shaker a little more than halfway with ice, and then muddle. Add rum, blood orange puree, and lime juice. Cover and shake, and pour into tall glass. Top with soda or Sprite. Stir and garnish with mint sprigs.

Yield: 1 serving

Bellinis Ristorante
6801 Cahaba Valley Road • Hoover, Alabama 35242
Phone: 205.981.5380 • ourbellinis.supportlocalflavor.com

Cherry Poppins Cocktail

Little Savannah · Chef/Owners Clif & Maureen Holt

1¾ ounces rye whiskey
¾ ounce sweet vermouth
Splash of Spiced Brandy
4 dashes cherry bitters

Spiced Brandy
750 milliliters brandy/cognac
½ split vanilla bean
6 whole cloves
1 whole star anise

Directions:
For the Spiced Brandy: Add split vanilla bean, cloves, and star anise to brandy or cognac. Place in a glass jar and let infuse for 3 days. Strain out cloves after 3 days. Store in the glass jar.

To make the cocktail: Combine all ingredients in a glass and stir well. Serve over ice.

Yield: 1 serving

Cucumber Mojito

Jinsei

4 large mint leaves
1 teaspoon granulated sugar
1 tablespoon peeled, diced cucumber
2 ounces rum
1 ounce Club Soda
3 ounces Sour Mix
1 cucumber slice

Sour Mix
2 cups granulated sugar
2 cups water
2 cups lime juice

Directions:
For the Sour Mix: In a small saucepan, whisk sugar and water together. Bring mixture to a boil
and whisk until sugar is completely dissolved. Remove from heat and add lime juice. Refrigerate
in an airtight container. Keeps up to 2 days.

In a glass tumbler, muddle mint, sugar, and cucumber well until flavors combine and mint oil
is released. Fill a glass to the rim with ice. Add rum, soda, and Sour Mix. Cover glass with metal
shaker and vigorously shake. Pour cocktail in a highball glass and garnish with cucumber slice
on rim.

Yield: 1 serving

Jinsei
1830 29th Avenue South • Homewood, Alabama 35209
Phone: 205.802.1440 • jinseisushi.com

Destin Cocktail

Five Bar

1¼ ounces Tito's vodka (or your favorite)
1½ ounces cranberry juice cocktail
¾ ounce fresh grapefruit juice
1 ounce Prosecco

Directions:
Fill a shaker with ice; add Tito's vodka, cranberry juice, and grapefruit juice. Shake and strain into a sugar-and-salt-rimmed martini glass. Top with Prosecco. Garnish with a grapefruit twist.

Yield: 1 serving

Five Bar Birmingham
744 29th Street South • Birmingham, Alabama 35233
Phone: 205.868.3841 • five-bar.com/birmingham

Eddie's Rose
Pale Eddie's Pour House

Eddie's Rose is a variation of the Jack Rose. Rather than using apple brandy as called for in the original recipe, we stay true to our roots by using apple moonshine for our spin on this classic cocktail.

2 ounces Apple Pie Moonshine from Firefly®
.75 ounces Housemade Grenadine (about 4 teaspoons)
.75 ounces fresh lime juice (about 4 teaspoons)
2 Dashes of Fee Brothers Old Fashioned Bitters (if unavailable, substitute Angostura Bitters)
Club soda
Lime wedge, for garnish

Housemade Grenadine
1 (16-ounce) bottle of POM 100% pomegranate juice
1 cup of sugar
Zest of one orange

Directions:
To make the Housemade Grenadine: Combine ingredients into a nonreactive saucepan. (stainless steel, non-aluminum) Bring to a boil. Strain with a fine sieve into a heatproof glass container like a Mason jar. Allow the syrup to cool in an ice bath or in a refrigerator. Will keep for 2 weeks, refrigerated.

To make the cocktail: Combine all ingredients into a shaker except for the soda. Shake with ice to combine ingredients. Strain into a pint-size Mason jar that has been filled with ice. Top cocktail off with club soda. Garnish with lime wedge.

Yield: 1 serving

Pale Eddie's Pour House
2308 2nd Avenue North • Birmingham, Alabama 35203
Phone: 205.542.5562 • paleeddiespourhouse.com

Tradicional Margarita

El Barrio Restaurante y Bar

Lime Mix Base
2 cups fresh lime juice
¾ cup sugar
2 cups water
1½ ounces Cazadores Reposado tequila
½ ounce Grand Marnier

Directions:
To prepare Lime Mix Base, bring sugar and water to boil. Chill and stir in lime juice.

Pour lime mix to taste into a shaker with ice. Add tequila and Grand Marnier and shake. Pour into a glass with salted rim. (Use kosher salt.)

Yield: 1 serving

El Barrio Restaurante y Bar
2211 2nd Avenue North • Birmingham, Alabama 35203
Phone: 205.868.3737 • elbarriobirmingham.com

Pickled Cherry Lime Rickey

Ollie Irene
James Beard Foundation Award Semi-Finalist

1 finger pickle juice (approximately
   3 teaspoons)
1 lime wedge
4 counts Hendricks Gin (approximately
   1½ ounces or 3 tablespoons)
2 tablespoons simple syrup
Pickled Cherries for garnish

Simple Syrup
½ cup granulated sugar
½ cup cool water

Pickled Cherries
3 cups water
2 cups red wine vinegar
2 cups sugar
2 star anise, whole
½ cinnamon stick
4 pieces allspice
4 whole cloves
2 quarts whole fresh cherries, washed

Directions:
For the Simple Syrup: Put the water and sugar in a small saucepan, stirring occasionally to dissolve the sugar. Bring to a boil. Remove from heat. Allow to cool completely. Pour into a jar. Will keep in the refrigerator for 1 week. Yield: ½ cup

For the Pickled Cherries: Combine all ingredients except the cherries in pot on stove. Bring to boil, let simmer for 30 seconds longer, turn off, and let cool. Put washed cherries in a glass or nonreactive container, pour brine over top, and refrigerate. You may use the cherries after a day, but they can stay in the brine indefinitely if refrigerated.

For the cocktail: In a cocktail shaker, squeeze the lime, drop it into the shaker, and muddle the lime wedge with the pickle juice. Add simple syrup and gin. Add ice to the shaker. Shake until well chilled. Strain and pour over ice in a rocks glass. Garnish with pickled cherries.

Yield: 1 cocktail

Ollie Irene
2713 Culver Road • Mountain Brook, Alabama 35223
Phone: 205.769.6034 • ollieirene.com

The Honeysuckle Rose
The Collins Bar

1¼ ounce Cathead Honeysuckle Vodka
¾ ounce Domaine de Canton ginger liqueur
½ ounce Aperol (Italian aperitif)
½ ounce lemon juice
½ ounce lime juice
¼ ounce simple syrup (equal parts sugar and water)
1 egg white
Lemon thyme (you may substitute regular thyme if necessary)

Directions:
Put all ingredients into a shaker tin, no ice, and shake vigorously. (It's called a "dry shake.")

Add ice, shake vigorously. (It's called a "wet shake.")

Strain into a coupe/martini glass. Garnish with the lemon thyme.

Yield: 1 serving

The Collins Bar
2125 2nd Avenue North • Birmingham, Alabama 35203
Phone: 205.323.7995 • collinsbirmingham.com

The Virgin Island Old Fashioned
The Collins Bar

Demerara Syrup
½ cup water
½ cup Demerara sugar

Cocktail
1½ ounces bourbon (such as Four Roses Yellow Label)
¼ ounce Cynar (Italian bitter liqueur)
¼ ounce Cruzan Blackstrap Rum
¼ ounce Demerara syrup
2 dashes Angostura bitters
Thick-sliced orange peel

Directions:
To prepare the Demerara Syrup: Add water and sugar to a saucepan. Stir. Bring to boil. Remove from heat, stirring to ensure sugar is completely dissolved. Allow to cool completely. Pour into a glass jar with a lid.

Combine all ingredients except orange peel in a mixing glass and stir to chill, mix, and dilute. Strain into an old-fashioned glass filled with ice or large cube.

Zest the peel over the drink. Flame the zest if desired.

Yield: 1 serving

Wine Loft Sazerac

The Wine Loft

A Sazerac is a variation of the classic Old Fashioned, and we have added our own flair for a truly delectable afternoon cocktail.

2 ounces Maker's Mark bourbon
¼ ounce Vanilla Brown Sugar Simple Syrup
3-4 dashes orange bitters (We make our own blood orange and grapefruit bitters, but the store-bought orange bitters will be close.)
Dash of Lucid Absinthe

Brown Sugar Simple Syrup
1 cup cool water
1 cup brown sugar
2 dashes pure vanilla extract

Directions:
To make the Brown Sugar Simple Syrup: In a pan, bring the water and sugar to a boil over high heat. Remove from heat; stir to dissolve the sugar. Add the vanilla. Allow to cool completely. Strain into a glass jar with a lid. Will keep for 1 week in the refrigerator.

For the cocktail: Put Absinthe in a rocks glass and roll the glass around to coat the inner surface. In a shaker, combine the bourbon, simple syrup, bitters, and 3-4 cubes of ice and stir. Pour into the coated rocks glass through a strainer and garnish with a blood orange twist.

Yield: 1 cocktail

The Wine Loft
2200 1st Avenue North #100 • Birmingham, Alabama 35203
Phone: 205.323.8228 • wineloftbham.com

Starters & Sides

Arancini Di Riso Balls (Fried Risotto Balls Stuffed with Mozzarella Cheese)

The J. Clyde

6 cups chicken stock
1½ cups Arborio rice
2 shallots, minced
¼ cup butter
¼ cup white wine
Salt and pepper, to taste
2 cups shredded mozzarella cheese
4 eggs, beaten
4 cups Panko bread crumbs
Oil for frying
2 ounces Parmesan-Reggiano

Directions:

For the risotto: Add butter to a large skillet, and stir in the shallots. Cook 1 minute. Add rice, stirring to coat with butter, about 2 minutes. When the rice has taken on a pale, golden color, pour in wine, stirring constantly until the wine is fully absorbed. Add ½ cup stock to the rice, and stir until the broth is absorbed. Continue adding broth ½ cup at a time, stirring continuously, until the liquid is absorbed, and the rice is al dente, about 15-20 minutes. Let risotto cool to room temperature.

To make the Fried Risotto Balls: When cool, scoop 2 ounces of risotto and flatten in the palm of your hand. Add a generous pinch of mozzarella to the center of the rice and form a ball with the risotto, making sure that the cheese is in the center of the ball. Chill risotto balls in refrigerator for 2 hours.

Preheat oil to 350°F in a large Dutch oven. While oil is heating, roll each ball in the beaten eggs and transfer to a bowl containing the bread crumbs. Coat each ball with bread crumbs and set aside. Fry each ball in oil for about 6 minutes, until golden brown and heated through. The cheese in the center of the ball should be melted when frying is complete.

Garnish with freshly grated Parmesan-Reggiano and serve with dipping sauce of your choice like marinara or pesto.

Yield: 8 pieces

The J. Clyde
1312 Cobb Lane • Birmingham, Alabama 35205
Phone: 205.939.1312 • jclyde.com

Ashley Mac's Famous Mac 'N Cheese

Ashley Mac's

½ cup butter
1 teaspoon salt
½ teaspoon pepper
½ cup flour
3½ cups milk
2 cups cooked elbow macaroni
16 ounces sharp cheddar cheese, shredded

Directions:
Preheat oven to 350°F.

Melt butter in saucepan. Add salt and pepper. Gradually whisk in flour, stirring constantly to prevent clumps. Gradually add milk and bring to a boil for 1 minute, stirring constantly to prevent burning. Layer macaroni, sauce, and cheese in a casserole dish. Bake at 350°F for 20 minutes.

Yield: 8 servings

Ashley Mac's
Cahaba Heights • 3147 Green Valley Road • Cahaba Heights, Alabama 35243
Inverness • 5299 Valleydale Road • Birmingham, Alabama 35242
Phone: 205.822.4142 • ashleymacs.com

Becky's Corn Muffins

Satterfield's

⅔ cup yellow-enriched cornmeal
1½ cups all-purpose flour
1¼ cup granulated sugar
1 tablespoon baking powder
1 teaspoon kosher salt
2¾ cups buttermilk
8 large eggs
¾ cup vegetable or peanut oil
3 ears yellow corn, shucked and kernels removed
3 green onions, finely chopped

Directions:
Preheat oven to 400°F.

Add the cornmeal, flour, sugar, baking powder, and salt to a large mixing bowl. Gently mix to combine. Add the buttermilk, eggs, and oil. Whisk until incorporated. Scrape the sides of the bowl and whisk for another 30 seconds. Stir in the corn and green onion.

Spray a small muffin pan with non-stick spray. Spoon the batter into the muffin wells. Place in the oven and cook for 17-20 minutes, until browned.

Yield: Approximately 2 dozen mini muffins

Satterfield's
3161 Cahaba Heights Road • Birmingham, Alabama 35243
Phone: 205.969.9690 • satterfieldsrestaurant.com

El Barrio Ceviche

El Barrio Restaurante y Bar

1 pound very fresh Gulf Shrimp or other fish
¾ cup fresh lime juice
¼ cup fresh orange juice
2 medium red onions, finely diced and rinsed (place in a sieve and run under hot water for
    45 seconds to remove the "hot, raw flavor"; refresh under cold water for 30 seconds)
2 fresh jalapeño or serrano chilies, stemmed, seeded and finely chopped (Add more or less
    depending on your taste.)
1 red bell pepper, stemmed, seeded, and finely diced
1 poblano pepper, stemmed, seeded, and finely diced
¼ cup of cilantro, washed and finely chopped
2 large avocados, diced
1 cup diced fresh pineapple or mango
Salt and pepper
Corn chips

Directions:

Peel shrimp and devein, if necessary. Using a sharp knife, cut shrimp in half lengthwise and then chop into small pieces. Place into a glass or other nonreactive bowl and mix in lime and orange juice. Cover and refrigerate 4-6 hours to allow shrimp to "cook."

Just before you plan to serve the ceviche, mix in the onions, bell peppers, Poblano, cilantro, and chilies. Season to taste. Dice avocado and season with salt and lime juice.

To serve, place on small plates for appetizers or into a bowl for dipping. Sprinkle with diced avocado, pineapple, mango, and cilantro. Serve with corn chips.

Yield: 4 servings as an appetizer or 8 as a dip

We use shrimp for our ceviche at El Barrio, but nearly any fresh seafood can be substituted. In fact, this recipe is a great kicking off point that can be adapted to suit both the ingredients on hand and your personal tastes.

El Barrio Restaurante y Bar
2211 2nd Avenue North • Birmingham, Alabama 35203
Phone: 205.868.3737 • elbarriobirmingham.com

Chipotle Spiced Pecans
El Barrio Restaurante y Bar

These sweet and spicy nuts are great on ice cream, as a snack, or a gift.

2 cups sugar
4 tablespoons kosher salt
5 pounds pecan halves
16 ounces honey
4 tablespoons ground cinnamon
2 teaspoons ground star anise
3 tablespoons ground chipotle

Directions:
Preheat oven to 325°F.

Mix together sugar and salt in a large mixing bowl and set aside.

Place pecans on a baking sheet and toast in oven for 8-10 minutes or until they begin to become fragrant.

Meanwhile combine honey, cinnamon, star anise, and chipotle in a saucepan large enough to comfortably hold the pecans; bring mixture to a gentle simmer. Add pecans and cook over low heat, 4-5 minutes, stirring until pecans are well coated.

Carefully pour pecans into the bowl with sugar-salt mixture and toss until completely coated and there is no more sugar loose in the bowl. Set aside to cool and dry.

Pack into airtight containers and store in a cool dry place.

Yield: 20 cups

El Barrio Restaurante y Bar
2211 2nd Avenue North • Birmingham, Alabama 35203
Phone: 205.868.3737 • elbarriobirmingham.com

Shrimp Saganaki

Dodiyo's · Chef George Sarris

3 pounds jumbo shrimp, peeled
¼ cup olive oil
2 white onions, thinly sliced
2 cloves fresh garlic, chopped
2 (28-ounce) cans plum tomatoes
1 cup dry white wine
2 teaspoons fresh oregano, chopped
Juice of 2 lemons plus zest
1½ cups crumbled feta cheese
4 cups cooked orzo

Directions:

Sauté shrimp in olive oil until just cooked through. Reserve 2 teaspoons olive oil, and set shrimp aside.

Sauté onions and garlic in 2 teaspoons olive oil. Add tomatoes and wine and cook over low heat for 30 minutes. Add oregano, lemon juice, and zest.

Add shrimp and stir in feta. Serve over orzo.

Yield: 4 servings

Eagle's Restaurant Large Lima Beans also Known as "Butter Beans"

Eagles Restaurant

2 pound bag of your favorite brand of large lima beans, rinsed and sorted
½ cup finely chopped onions
½ cup finely chopped bell pepper
2 cloves finely chopped garlic
1 tablespoon black pepper
1 tablespoon salt
2 tablespoons sugar
2 tablespoons vegetable oil or ½ stick of butter if you prefer
Whole okra (optional)

Directions:
Wash and let the beans soak while you prepare remaining ingredients. You have an option of adding a meat of your choice for seasoning. It could be turkey wings, smoked neck bones, ham, chicken, or bacon.

Wash and rinse beans off, sort through, and remove any debris. Place the beans and remaining ingredients except the okra into a stock pot. Add water to cover your beans, plus 2 more inches of water. Cook on high heat and bring to a boil. Keep an eye on the pot, occasionally stir, and never let your water get too low. Monitor and add water, as needed, to maintain 2 inches of water above the beans.

At the 1½ hour mark, reduce the heat to medium, and let simmer for 30 additional minutes. If using, add okra approximately 15 minutes before the beans are done. Check for tenderness. Taste and adjust seasonings for personal preference.

Total cooking time is approximately 2 hours, depending on the bean you use.

Yield: 6-8 servings

Eagles Restaurant
2610 16th Street North • Birmingham, Alabama 35204
Phone: 205.320.0099 • eaglesrestaurant.com

Farm Egg and Kale Tartine

Chez Fonfon · Chef Frank Stitt

James Beard Foundation Award Winner

Egg Salad

9 soft-boiled farm eggs
1 finely minced shallot
1 tablespoon chopped chervil
1 tablespoon sliced chives
1 tablespoon coarse-grain mustard
1 lemon
3 tablespoons aioli
Salt and black pepper

½ pound Tuscan kale
2 thinly sliced radishes
2 slices of Wild Yeast Sourdough bread

Carrot-Cider Vinaigrette

2 finely minced shallots
1 tablespoon chopped thyme
½ cup diced carrots
¼ cup cider vinegar
2 tablespoons coarse-grain mustard
1 cup extra-virgin olive oil

Directions:

To make Egg Salad: Bring a pot of water to a slight simmer, and gently place the eggs into the pot, allowing them to cook for 7½ minutes. Immediately transfer the eggs to a container of water and ice, "shock water," to stop them from cooking any further.

Tip: When boiling eggs always try to allow them to come to room temperature before putting them into boiling water to allow for more consistent cooking time. Always leave the cooked eggs in the shock water until you are ready to peel them; this will make the shells easier to remove.

Coarsely chop the peeled eggs and combine them with remaining ingredients; add salt and black pepper to taste. Place in a fridge until ready to serve.

To make Carrot-Cider Vinaigrette: In a large mixing bowl combine the shallot, thyme, carrot, cider vinegar, and grain mustard. Allow these ingredients to set for about 10 minutes before slowly whisking in the olive oil, salt, and black pepper. Taste for seasoning.

To assemble, coarsely chop kale and toss it with the vinaigrette, adding salt and pepper as needed.

Chez Fonfon
2007 11th Avenue South • Birmingham, Alabama 35205
Phone: 205.939.3221 • fonfonbham.com

Over a medium-hot grill, toast the Wild-Yeast Sourdough. Spread a generous layer of the egg salad over the toast, and then top it with the kale slaw. Cut into four equal portions and garnish with the sliced radishes.

Yield: 4 portions

Flammkuchen - Crispy Thin Crust Pizza with Gruyere and Bacon

The Wine Loft

Flammkuchen-(translates to flaming cake). A common offering in Southwest Germany and the Alsace region of France, it is their version of a pizza. Made with a thin crust and créme fraîche instead of tomato based sauce, it is light and delicious.

1 - pizza dough to make a very thin 12-inch shell (from scratch, store bought, or get one from your favorite pizza place)
¼ cup créme fraîche (purchase or make from scratch)
¼ cup grated Gruyere cheese
¼ cooked bacon lardons (diced bacon, cooked)
¼ cup thinly sliced onions
¼ cup banana pepper slices
½ teaspoon caraway seeds

Directions:
Preheat oven (preferably with a pizza stone) to 450°F.

Roll out pizza dough to make a very thin crust; then uniformly spread the créme fraîche to coat the bread and sprinkle the Gruyere across the surface. Distribute the rest of your topping across the surface and bake on a pizza stone until edges are nice and brown, about 5-10 minutes, depending upon your oven.

Yield: 1 pizza

Full Moon Macaroni and Cheese

Full Moon Bar-B-Que

1 cup whole milk
½ cup solid margarine
Pinch of white pepper
Pinch of salt
1 cup shredded American cheese
3 cups elbow macaroni noodles, cooked and drained

Directions:

Preheat oven to 350°F.

Bring milk to a boil. Add margarine, salt, and white pepper. Slowly add cheese to pot while stirring constantly over medium heat. Add to macaroni noodles, stirring until noodles are coated. Transfer to a 2-quart baking dish. Cover and bake for 25 minutes at 350°F.

Yield: 6-8 servings

Full Moon Bar-B-Que
The Original/Southside • 525 25th Street South • Phone: 205.324.1007
Hoover • 2000 Patton Chapel Road • Phone: 205.822.6666
Inverness • 4635 US Highway 280 • Phone: 205.991.7328
Valley Avenue • 337 Valley Avenue • Phone: 205.945.9997
For additional locations and information: fullmoonbbq.com

Full Moon
BAR-B-QUE

Greek Spanakopita Spinach Pie
The Red Cat

1 box Phyllo pastry sheets (#7, if possible), 14"x18" at room temperature
4 tablespoons vegetable oil, plus a little more for sautéing the onions
½ stick salted butter
4 ounces cream cheese
34 ounces frozen spinach
10 ounces frozen collard greens
2 ounces dill, chopped
1 small to medium onion, diced
½ teaspoon salt
½ teaspoon pepper
16 ounces feta cheese, crumbled
6 eggs, lightly beaten

Directions:

Sauté the onions in a large stovetop pan until translucent. Add in the spinach and collard greens. Heat until completely thawed and hot throughout, but without burning. Remove from heat. Stir in the salt, pepper, and dill. Place the cream cheese into the hot spinach mixture so that it can melt. After the cream cheese has melted and you have stirred it in evenly, set aside to cool.

Meanwhile, in a separate large container, mix together the feta cheese and the eggs. Pour this into the cooled spinach mixture and combine all the ingredients. This is the stuffing of the spanakopita.

Melt the half stick of butter. Pour in the 4 ounces of vegetable oil and mix the two together. This will be the mixture with which you will brush the Phyllo dough.

Spray the bottoms and inner sides of a large rectangular baking pan (we use a 12"x17"x2") with cooking spray. Open the box of Phyllo sheets and lay flat on the counter next to the pan. Carefully lay the sheets onto the pan, one by one, brushing each with the butter mixture as you go. You will lay about ⅔ of the sheets before adding the spinach mixture. The trick is to lay one sheet on the bottom flat, then lay the other sheets so that one side of them extends up the sides of the pan and falls over the edge about one inch. This keeps the spinach mixture from touching the side of the metal pan.

With the Phyllo sheets still draped over the side of the pan, scoop the spinach mixture into the pan and spread evenly. Fold the loose sheets of the Phyllo over onto the top of the spinach mixture. Now lay the rest of the Phyllo sheets over the top of the spinach mixture, brushing each one as you go. If the sheets are slightly bigger than the pan, just fold over the extra back onto the sheet.

Preheat the oven to 350°F. While the oven is heating up, score the top of the uncooked spanakopita with a sharp knife according to the size pieces that you want. We score 12 equal pieces. Cook for about 42 minutes. The top should be browned, but not burnt. If the pie has expanded in some places during cooking, it will return to normal once it cools.

Let the pie thoroughly cool. Serve by microwaving for 1 minute, and then toasting for a few minutes on each side. Serve with fresh tomatoes and hummus.

Yield: 12 pieces or 24 if you make bite-size portions

Housemade Ricotta and Charred Tomato Crostini

Bettola · Chef James Lewis

James Beard Foundation Award Semi-Finalist

Housemade Ricotta
1 gallon whole milk
½ teaspoon citric acid
½ teaspoon sea salt

Crostini
½ cup olive oil
1-2 cloves garlic
8-10 slices slightly stale Italian or French bread, thinly sliced

Tomatoes
16-20 small cherry tomatoes
1 teaspoon olive oil
Pinch sea salt, or to taste
Fresh basil leaves, torn into pieces
Black pepper (optional)
Aged balsamic vinegar (optional)

Directions:
To prepare Housemade Ricotta: Heat whole milk to 360°F; then remove pan and let cool. Add ½ teaspoon citric acid and ½ teaspoon sea salt and stir. Chill and strain with linen or double-lined cheesecloth; drain to catch whey.

To make Crostini: Heat ½ cup of oil on low in a cast iron skillet or pan. Add one smashed garlic clove and heat on low 4-5 minutes. Remove oil and garlic from skillet. Reserve oil in a heatproof container.

Return a small amount of oil and heat skillet to medium.

Add several slices of bread into pan and toast until lightly browned on each side. Remove slices when they have reached desired level of crispness. Add a small amount of garlic oil back into skillet, and continue toasting until lightly browned.

Bettola
2901 2nd Avenue South • Birmingham, Alabama 35233
Phone: 205.731.6499 • bettolarestaurant-hub.com

To prepare Tomatoes: Lightly rub on olive oil and sea salt. Char them in hot cast-iron skillet over medium-high heat before toasting the bread for crostini, or roast them under a broiler to blister the tomato while toasting the bread. Once tomatoes are charred or blistered, smash the tomatoes to break them up a bit. If they are sweeter, leave them whole.

To assemble, spread ricotta on bread. Top with charred tomatoes. Garnish with fresh basil, season with sea salt, olive oil, and a pinch of black pepper and balsamic vinegar if desired.

Tip: When making the Housemade Ricotta, it helps to put cheesecloth over a colander and let it slowly drain. After you have strained the ricotta, remove it from the linen. At this point you can mix in your choice of seasoning such as fresh herbs, citrus zest, honey, or bacon; adjust the seasoning to fit the dish you are serving the ricotta with. For smoother cheese, pulse in food processor until it has reached your desired consistency.

Yield: 8-10 servings

Orange & Blue Oyster Poppers with Blue Cheese Dipping Sauce

Dixie Fish Company

2 teaspoons salt
1 teaspoon black pepper
2 cups all-purpose flour
1-2 ounces Crystal hot sauce
4 tablespoons honey
12 ounces clarified butter
36 oysters
Cooking oil
1 cup blue cheese dressing, store bought

Directions:

Add salt and pepper to all-purpose flour to make seasoned flour; set aside.

Place Crystal hot sauce and honey in a blender. Heat butter to 140°F and pour slowly into blender through the opening on top with blender on low speed. Then blend at medium speed for a few seconds. Set hot sauce mixture aside.

Drain excess liquid off oysters and dredge in the seasoned flour. Shake to remove excess flour and set aside.

Add enough oil to skillet to pan-fry. Over medium-high heat, bring the oil up to 350°F, or you can also check the heat by dropping a little flour in the oil to make sure you are ready to fry. Add oysters and fry until golden brown and crispy. Remove from oil and place on paper towel to get rid of excess grease.

Toss oysters in a bowl with some of the hot sauce mixture. Serve in an oyster dish or on the half shell. Use blue cheese dressing as a dipping sauce.

Yield: 6 servings (about 6 oysters per serving)

Dixie Fish Company
101 Resource Center Parkway • Birmingham, Alabama 35242
Phone: 205.924.3493 • dixiefish.com

Pimento Cheese

Jim 'N Nick's

This spicy cheese spread is great troweled into a celery rib, slathered on a burger, or spooned onto a saltine, then topped with our spicy pork hot link.

1 pound grated cheddar cheese
1¼ cups mayonnaise
½ teaspoon hot sauce (such as Tabasco)
½ teaspoon cayenne pepper
10 ounces fire-roasted red peppers

Directions:
Mix ingredients; then cover and chill to mingle the flavors.

Yield: About 2 cups

Squash Croquettes
Fife's Restaurant

4 medium-size yellow squash
2 small onions
½ pound butter
3 eggs, well beaten
3 cups saltine crackers, crushed
½ cup cracker meal
1 tablespoon salt
1 tablespoon black pepper
2 tablespoons sugar
½ cup vegetable oil, for frying

Directions:
Wash and clean squash.

Slice squash about ½-inch thick and boil until soft. Allow to drain thoroughly.

Sauté 2 small onions in a sauce pan with ½ pound butter. Remove from heat and let cool.

When cooled, place squash, onions, and butter in a large bowl. Add together eggs, crackers, cracker meal, salt, pepper, and sugar, and continue to mix until all ingredients are evenly saturated.

Roll into medium-size balls.

Deep fry on medium heat until golden brown.

Yield: 4-6 servings

Fife's Restaurant
2321 4th Avenue North • Birmingham, Alabama 35203
Phone: 205.254.9167

Taramasalata Dip
Nabeel's Café & Market

8 ounces Tarama (You can find Tarama at international stores. It is also called Carp Roe.)
6-7 thick slices stale white bread, French or Italian, crust removed
8 ounces extra virgin olive oil plus ½ tablespoon
1 tablespoon red wine vinegar
2 lemons
1 medium-size white onion, finely chopped
Kalamata olives for garnish

Directions:
Pour over just enough water to wet the bread. Squeeze out as much water as possible and leave on absorbent kitchen paper towels to dry thoroughly. Once dry, add it to the bowl of a food processor along with the onion, Tarama, lemon juice, vinegar, and sugar.

Scrape down the sides of the container. With the processor running, gradually stream in the olive oil through the feeder tube. The oil must be added slowly enough so that it forms an emulsion. Taste and add a little more vinegar, oil, and lemon juice, if necessary. (If it is salty tasting or fishy smelling, add more lemon juice and oil very slowly.) The finished consistency should be something like softly whipped cream, just firm enough to mound slightly when dropped from a spoon. The dip will get firmer as it chills.

Scrape into a serving bowl and cover tightly. Chill for several hours before serving. Garnish with a few Kalamata olives. Serve with crusty bread or pita wedges.

Yield: 6-8 servings

Nabeel's Café & Market
1706 Oxmoor Road • Homewood, Alabama 35209
Phone: 205.879.9292 • nabeels.com

OUZO
METAXA

Tempura Zucchini Blossom Recipe
FoodBar · Chef George McMillian

Tempura
1 egg yolk
1 cup cornstarch
1 cup rice flour
Soda water (cold)
5-6 ice cubes
½ cup all-purpose flour (reserve for frying)

Zucchini Blossoms
½ pound shrimp, peeled and deveined
¼ cup butter

½ cup white wine
¼ cup shallots
4 cups breadcrumbs (use day-old brioche
    for best results)
4 tablespoons minced parsley
2 tablespoons lemon zest
Salt and pepper to taste
½ cup melted butter
10-12 large zucchini blossoms
All-purpose flour
Oil

Directions:
To make Tempura: Combine egg yolk, cornstarch, and rice flour, and add enough soda water to reach consistency of a pancake batter. Add 5-6 ice cubes; cover and refrigerate.

Sauté shrimp in butter, white wine, and shallots. Allow to cool before roughly chopping.

Combine shrimp, breadcrumbs, parsley, lemon zest, salt and pepper, and mix thoroughly. Add butter to breadcrumb mixture and combine. Carefully stuff zucchini blossoms with breadcrumb mixture (enough to fill blossoms to the top). Fold petals in from the top and firmly mold in the palm of your hand. Cover and chill in refrigerator at least 1 hour or as long as overnight.

Dredge stuffed blossom in all-purpose flour and coat evenly. Dip blossom into tempura, coating all sides. Submerge in 350°F oil for 2-3 minutes, turning occasionally. After frying, transfer to plate lined with paper towel and sprinkle with salt. Slice in half lengthwise for plate presentation.

Note: Stir tempura mixture between each blossom 'dunking.' Otherwise, the cornstarch sinks to the bottom of the batter and you won't achieve the desired light consistency. Squash is interchangeable for the zucchini blossoms, depending on which is readily available.

Yield: 10-12 blossoms

FoodBar
3156 Heights Village • Vestavia Hills, Alabama 35243
Phone: 205.876.8100 • foodbarbham.com

Salads, Soup & Sandwiches

Dreamla
BAR   B
S·A·U·
"Ain't no

BBQ Ham Shooter Sandwich featuring Dreamland Bar-B-Que Sauce and Seasoning Shake

Dreamland Bar-B-Que

3 cups hickory smoked ham, ½-inch cubes
¾ cup red onion, julienned
1½ teaspoons Dreamland™ Shake
¾ cup Wickles™ Pickles, quartered
1 cup Dreamland™ BBQ Sauce
4 (6-inch) crusty hoagie buns, sliced ¾ of the way through, horizontally, and hollowed out

Directions:

In a large sauté pan, heat 2 tablespoons of oil over medium-high heat. Add onion and cook for 3 minutes until soft. Stir in cubed ham and season with Dreamland™ Shake seasoning.

Add Wickles™ and Dreamland™ BBQ Sauce, stirring to combine. Reduce heat to simmer and cook an additional 2 minutes.

Fill each hoagie bun with 1 cup of filling, ensuring that bun encloses all of the filling. Remove any excess. Heat a clean skillet over medium-high heat.

Place hoagies in hot pan and briefly press down with a press or another pan. Flip over and press again. Repeat with all sandwiches.

To serve, slice horizontally.

Yield: 4 servings

Dreamland Bar-B-Que
1427 14th Avenue, South • Birmingham, Alabama 35205
Phone: 205.933.2133 • dreamlandbbq.com

Beer Battered Vegetables with a Spicy Dipping Sauce

GaBriella's Bistro and Art Gallery

Dipping Sauce

1 cup ranch dressing

1 cup sour cream

¼ cup tiger sauce

¼ cup finely chopped green onion

2 tablespoons Dijon mustard

1 teaspoon pepper flakes

Juice of one lemon

Beer Batter

1 cup flour

1⅛ teaspoon baking powder

1 cup beer

1 egg

2 teaspoons salt

1 teaspoon garlic powder

1 teaspoon Old Bay Seasoning

¾ teaspoon pepper

Vegetables

12 large okra pods, sliced length wise

12 large button mushrooms

1 pound blanched whole green beans

2 large white potatoes, cut in large dices and blanched

2 large green tomatoes, cut into ½-inch-thick slices

4-6 cups cooking oil for deep frying (amount depends on the size of the pot)

Directions:

To prepare Dipping Sauce: Combine ranch dressing and next 6 ingredients, stirring well. Set aside.

To prepare Beer Batter: Combine flour and baking powder, stirring well. Add beer, egg, and next 4 ingredients, stirring until combined.

In a large Dutch oven or heavy pot, add the cooking oil, filling just under the halfway point and fit the pot with a cooking thermometer. Add the cooking oil and heat to 350°F.

To prepare Vegetables: Dip vegetables in tempura batter and fry in oil until golden brown, about 3-5 minutes. Remove from cooking oil and drain on paper towels. Arrange on a tray and serve with dipping sauce.

Yield: 4-6 servings

GaBriella's Bistro and Art Gallery
317 17th Street North • Birmingham, Alabama 35203
Phone: 205.566.2291

Mushroom and Brie Soup

Crestwood Café

½ cup butter
¾ cup of chopped celery
1 cup onion, diced
½ cup garlic, chopped
¾ cup flour
3 pounds fresh mushrooms, sliced (I use oyster, shiitake, and baby portabella.)
2 cups sherry (not cooking sherry)
3 cups vegetable stock (You can use Knorr base and water.)
2 cups heavy cream
4 cups half-and-half
2 cups shredded Brie cheese
3 sprigs fresh thyme leaves, minced
White pepper and Tony Chachere's seasoning, to taste

Directions:

Melt the butter in soup pot over medium-low heat. Add the onions, celery, and garlic, and cook until soft. Whisk in the flour and cook until a light roux is made. Add the thyme, white pepper, and Tony Chachere's seasoning. Deglaze the pot with 1 cup sherry,* and let it come to a boil. Add the vegetable stock and half-and-half. Bring to a boil; then reduce the heat and simmer for 10 minutes.

Allow the mixture to cool slightly before adding it to a blender. You can also use an immersion blender. This step is not necessary; it depends on the consistency you are looking for.

Add the mushrooms, and let mixture come to a boil again. Reduce heat and simmer for 20 minutes. Stir in the brie and mix through. Once mixed, add the heavy cream and the sherry; let simmer for 10 more minutes, then enjoy.

Garnish with chopped flat leafed parsley or green onion tops for a little color.

Yield: 12-15 servings based on portion size

*Note: To prevent flames, always remove the pan from the heat when adding alcohol.

Crestwood Café
5512 Crestwood Boulevard • Birmingham, Alabama 35212
Phone: 205.595.0300 • crestwoodcafe.com

Hotbox Cucumber Salad

Hotbox

Salad

2 English cucumbers, halved lengthwise,
seeds removed, then cut half-moon
shapes of various sizes

½ cup carrots, shredded

¼ cup red onion, shaved (a mandolin
works best)

2 cups Napa cabbage, dark leaves
removed, cut lengthwise, then cut
into ½ inch strips

1 cup cherry tomatoes, halved

6 mint leaves, torn

12 springs cilantro, ends removed, leaves
rough chopped, stems chopped fine

4 green onions (scallions) cut into small
rounds

1 tablespoon fried garlic

Dressing

¼ cup fresh lime juice (about 3 medium
limes)

1 tablespoon palm sugar

2 tablespoons rice wine vinegar

2 tablespoons fish sauce

1 tablespoon olive oil

1 pinch kosher salt

Directions:

For the Dressing: Assemble all the ingredients for the dressing in a bowl. Whisk until the sugar is dissolved. Set aside. (Keeps in the refrigerator for up to 3 days.)

To serve: In a large mixing bowl, combine the cucumber, carrot, and red onion. Add ¾ of the dressing and toss well for 2-3 minutes. Add cabbage, tomatoes, and herbs and toss briefly.

Use a slotted spoon to transfer the salad to your serving dish. Pour remaining dressing around the serving plate; salad should be loose and saucy. Salad should be served immediately after dressing. Garnish with fried garlic and extra herbs as desired.

Note: In Birmingham, you may find the palm sugar, rice wine vinegar, and fish sauce at most well-stocked stores like Whole Foods or at an Asian market like Chai's Oriental Food Store or Red Pearl/Super Oriental Market.

Yield: 4 servings

Field Pea Salad with Cucumber, Sweet Corn, Tomatoes, and Balsamic Vinaigrette

Brick & Tin

1 shallot
⅓ cup balsamic vinegar
1 cup extra-virgin olive oil
Salt and black pepper to taste
3 ears fresh yellow corn, husks and threads removed
2 cups cooked field peas (pink-eyed, crowder, or lady)
1 cup halved cherry tomatoes
1 cup diced cucumber
2 leaves fresh basil

Directions:
Preheat oven to 400°F.

To make Balsamic Vinaigrette: Finely mince shallot and place in a medium mixing bowl. Cover with balsamic vinegar and allow to macerate for 20 minutes. Set aside 2 tablespoons of olive oil. Then slowly drizzle in remainder, whisking to create a vinaigrette. Season to taste with salt and pepper. Set aside.

To cook the corn: Coat corn lightly with reserved 2 tablespoons olive oil and season with salt and pepper. Place on a baking sheet pan and roast 20 minutes. Remove and set aside to cool. Once cooled, shave the kernels of the cobs with a knife and set aside.

In a mixing bowl, combine peas, corn, tomatoes, and cucumber and stir to mix. Tear basil leaves into small pieces and add to the pea mixture. Add enough of the vinaigrette to coat everything, and season with salt and pepper. Serve cold or at room temperature.

Yield: 6 servings

Brick & Tin
Downtown • 214 20th Street North • Phone: 205.297.8636
Mountain Brook Village • 2901 Cahaba Road • Phone: 205.502.7971
brickandtin.com

Cioppino
The Fish Market Restaurant

4 large garlic cloves, minced
2 medium onions, finely chopped
1 Turkish bay leaf or ½ California bay leaf
1 teaspoon dried oregano, crumbled
1 teaspoon dried, hot red pepper flakes
¼ cup olive oil
1 green bell pepper, diced
2 tablespoons tomato paste
1½ cups dry red wine
1 (28-32-ounces) can whole plum tomatoes (Drain, reserve juice, and chop.)
1 cup bottled clam juice
1 cup chicken broth
1 King Crab Leg or other large crab leg
1½ teaspoons salt
½ teaspoon black pepper
18 small (2-inch) hard-shelled clams (1½ pounds) such as littlenecks, scrubbed
1 pound skinless red snapper or halibut fillets, cut into 1½-inch pieces
1 pound large shrimp (16 to 20 count), shelled (tails and bottom segment of shells left intact)
    and deveined
¾ pound sea scallops, tough muscle removed from side of each if necessary
¼ cup finely chopped fresh, flat-leaf parsley
3 tablespoons finely chopped fresh basil
Garnish: shredded fresh basil leaves and small whole leaves

Directions:
Cook garlic, onions, bay leaf, oregano, and red pepper flakes in oil in an 8-quart heavy pot over moderate heat, stirring until onions are softened, about 5 minutes. Stir in bell pepper and tomato paste and cook, stirring 1 minute. Add wine and boil until reduced by about half, 5-6 minutes. Add tomatoes with their juice, clam juice, and chicken broth. Simmer, covered, 30 minutes. Season with salt and pepper.

While stew is simmering, hack crab leg through shell into 2-3-inch pieces with a large heavy knife. Add crab pieces and clams to stew and simmer, covered, until clams just open, 5-10 minutes, checking every minute after 5 minutes and transferring opened clams to a bowl with tongs or a slotted spoon. (Discard any unopened clams after 10 minutes.)

The Fish Market Birmingham
612 22nd Street South • Birmingham, Alabama 35233
Phone: 205.322.3330 • thefishmarket.net

Lightly season fish fillets, shrimp, and scallops with salt and add to stew. Then simmer, covered, until just cooked through, about 5 minutes. Discard bay leaf; then return clams to pot and gently stir in parsley and basil.

Serve Cioppino immediately in large soup bowls with sourdough bread or focaccia.

Yield: 6-8 portions, based on serving size

Ginger Lime Shrimp Salad
Ollie Irene
James Beard Foundation Award Semi-Finalist

¼ cup peeled ginger
½ cup rice wine vinegar
½ cup fish sauce (found in international
    or Asian aisle of grocery store)
2 tablespoons granulated sugar
1 pound Gulf Shrimp, 21-25 count
    (4 shrimp for each portion)
1 lemon
2 bay leaves
1 tablespoon whole black peppercorns
2 teaspoons kosher salt
3 limes, juice only

½ tablespoon Thai chili, finely diced (can
    substitute a jalapeno if necessary)
1 carrot, peeled and julienned
1 cucumber, peeled and julienned
½ daikon radish, peeled and julienned
¼ red onion, peeled and julienned
9 basil leaves, chiffonade (use Thai basil
    if possible)
4 scallions, chopped
3 tablespoons cilantro leaves, coarsely
    chopped
3 tablespoons mint leaves, coarsely chopped
¼ cup roasted peanuts, coarsely chopped –
    for garnish

Directions:

For the dressing: Put ginger, vinegar, and fish sauce in a blender, and blend on high speed. Strain liquid through a fine sieve or cheesecloth into a sauce pan and add sugar. Bring the liquid to a boil until sugar dissolves. Remove from heat. Transfer liquid to a bowl and let cool in refrigerator.

While dressing is cooling, poach the shrimp. To poach, put 4 quarts of cool water into a Dutch oven or large pot with a lid. Squeeze juice from the lemon and drop the halves into the pot. Stir in black peppercorns, bay leaves, and salt; bring to a boil over medium-high heat. Add the shrimp. Cover and let stand 5 minutes or until shrimp just turns pink. Remove the shrimp from the liquid; peel and devein. Set aside in refrigerator. (For variation, roast, grill, fry, or sauté the shrimp.)

To assemble: In a salad bowl, toss together the carrot, cucumber, red onion, daikon, basil, scallion, cilantro, and mint. Stir lime juice and chili into the cooled ginger liquid. Add the dressing and the shrimp to the vegetables; toss together. Garnish with chopped peanuts.

Yield: 6 servings

Ollie Irene
2713 Culver Road • Mountain Brook, Alabama 35223
Phone: 205.769.6034 • ollieirene.com

Grilled Fish Reuben with Crunchy Slaw

26 · Chef/Owner George Reis

Sweet Slaw Sauce
1½ cups mayonnaise
½ cup sugar
1½ lemons, juiced
1½ limes, juiced
1½ oranges, juiced

Crunchy Slaw
¼ head of green cabbage
⅛ head of red cabbage
2 carrots, shredded
½ cup Sweet Slaw Sauce

Remoulade
½ cup mayonnaise
¼ cup ketchup
1 teaspoon whole-grain mustard
Sprig of thyme
¼ teaspoon minced garlic
1 tablespoon capers
1 teaspoon dill

4 (6-7 ounce) tilapia fillets
Greek seasoning
Butter
8 slices rye bread
8 slices dill havarti cheese

Directions:
Prepare Sweet Slaw Sauce.

Prepare Crunchy Slaw and Remoulade.

Season tilapia with Greek seasoning. Grill fish 2-3 minutes on each side.

Coat one side of each bread slice with butter and top each slice with one slice cheese. Toast bread until cheese melts. Spread remoulade on bread. Top 4 bread slices evenly with slaw. Top slaw with one tilapia fillet, and top with remaining 4 bread slices.

Yield: 4 sandwiches

Honey Soy Sauce Dressing Over Salad Greens

Carrigan's Public House

Honey Soy Sauce
½ cup sugar
½ cup honey
1½ cups soy sauce

House Vinaigrette
1 cup red wine vinegar
1 tablespoon minced garlic
⅛ cup fresh thyme
1 tablespoon honey
½ tablespoon dried oregano
1½ tablespoons salt
1½ teaspoons black pepper
2 cups blended oil
1½ shallots, diced small

Directions:
For the Honey Soy Sauce: Combine all ingredients in a saucepan. Simmer on low heat for 20 minutes, and chill.

For the House Vinaigrette: Combine all ingredients, including the honey soy sauce; whisk well. Serve over a green salad. Add pan-seared grouper or any other fish if you like.

Yield: 5 cups

Hot and Hot Tomato Salad

Hot and Hot Fish Club · Chef Chris Hastings

James Beard Foundation Award Winner

Salad
6 large beefsteak tomatoes
2 large, golden delight tomatoes
2 large rainbow tomatoes
¾ cup plus 3 tablespoons Balsamic Vinaigrette (below), divided
1½ teaspoons kosher salt
¾ teaspoon freshly ground black pepper
1 smoked ham hock
1 large onion, peeled and quartered
1 fresh thyme sprig
6 ounces (1 cup) fresh field peas such as black-eye, pink-eye, crowder, or butter beans
2 tablespoons peanut oil
3 ears yellow corn, husked
6 slices Applewood smoked bacon, cooked until crisp
¾ cup chive dressing (below)
6 tablespoons chiffonade of fresh basil
½ pint sweet 100 tomatoes (tiny current tomatoes can be substituted)

Okra
4 cups vegetable oil
30 pieces whole baby okra
¼ cup whole-milk buttermilk
¼ cup corn flour
¼ cup corn meal
¼ cup all-purpose flour
1 teaspoon kosher salt, divided
½ teaspoon freshly ground black pepper, divided

Directions:
To prepare the Salad: Core and slice the beefsteak, golden delight, and rainbow tomatoes into ¼ -inch thick slices. Toss the tomatoes with ¾ cup of the vinaigrette. Season the tomatoes with the salt and pepper, and set aside at room temperature to marinate until ready to serve.

Hot and Hot Fish Club
2180 11th Court South • Birmingham, Alabama 35205
Phone: 205.933.5474 • hotandhotfishclub.com

Combine the ham hock, onion, thyme, and field peas in a medium stock pot with enough cold water to cover the beans. Bring the peas to a simmer and cook until just tender, 12-15 minutes, stirring occasionally. Remove from the heat, drain, and cool. Remove and discard the ham hock, onion quarters, and thyme sprig. Place the cooled peas in a mixing bowl and set aside.

Shave the kernels off the corn cobs, discarding the silk hairs. Heat the peanut oil in a large skillet over medium-high heat. Add the corn kernels and cook until tender, 8-10 minutes. Season the corn with salt and pepper to taste, and remove from the heat and cool slightly. Toss the corn kernels with the cooked field peas and the remaining 3 tablespoons of vinaigrette. Set the pea mixture aside to marinate at room temperature until ready to serve.

To prepare the Okra: Pour the vegetable oil into a deep-sided skillet to a depth of 3-inches. (Alternately, a deep fryer can be filled with vegetable oil.) Preheat the oil to 350°F.

Trim the okra stems and place okra pods in a small bowl with the buttermilk. Toss until well coated.

Combine the corn flour, cornmeal, all-purpose flour, salt, and pepper in medium size bowl. Drain the okra from the buttermilk and toss in the cornmeal mixture. Shake off any excess cornmeal mixture. Place the okra in the preheated vegetable oil and fry for 2-3 minutes, or until golden. Remove okra from the hot oil with a slotted spoon and drain on a paper towel-lined plate. Season the okra with the remaining salt and pepper if needed. Keep warm until ready to serve.

To serve: Arrange each of the different types of sliced tomatoes on 6 plates. Place the whole sweet 100 tomatoes around the sliced tomatoes. Divide the pea and corn mixture evenly among plates on top of the tomatoes. Arrange 5 pieces of fried okra around each plate and place 1 slice of crispy bacon on the top of each salad. Drizzle 1-2 tablespoons of the chive dressing over the tops of each salad, and garnish each with 1 tablespoon of basil chiffonade. Serve immediately.

Balsamic Vinaigrette:

½ cup extra-virgin olive oil

½ cup olive oil

1 cup finely chopped fresh chives

1 cup balsamic vinegar

½ cup chopped green onions

¼ teaspoon kosher salt

⅛ teaspoon freshly ground black pepper

Directions:
Whisk together all of the ingredients in a large bowl. The vinaigrette can be used immediately or stored in an airtight container in the refrigerator for up to five days. Be sure to bring the chilled vinaigrette to room temperature, and whisk well before serving. Makes 2 cups.

continued on next page

Chive Dressing
1 small garlic clove, peeled and finely minced
6 tablespoons finely chopped fresh chives
1 large egg yolk
2 tablespoons fresh lemon juice
½ teaspoon kosher salt
¼ teaspoon freshly ground black pepper
1 cup olive oil
¼ cup homemade créme fraîche
   (or store bought)

Directions:
Combine the garlic and chives in small bowl. Add egg yolk, lemon juice, salt, and pepper and whisk to combine. Add the olive oil in a thin, steady stream, while whisking vigorously. This should create an emulsion. Whisk in the créme fraîche. You may need to add a drop or two of water if dressing is too thick. Cover and chill the dressing for at least 20 minutes before serving. This dressing will keep refrigerated in an airtight container for up to two days. Makes about 1¼ cups.

Yield: 6 servings

Recipe copyright Chef Chris Hastings

Cole Slaw
Jim 'N Nick's

This slaw is perfect as a side dish or added to a pulled-pork sandwich.

1 (2-pound) head green cabbage, quartered, cored, cut crosswise into ⅛-inch thick slices
    (about 14 cups)
1¼ cups apple cider vinegar
1 cup sugar
1 cup peeled, grated carrot
4 green onions, thinly sliced (scallions)
¼ cup mayonnaise
Salt and pepper to taste

Directions:
Place cabbage in large bowl. Combine vinegar and sugar, stirring until sugar is dissolved. Add to cabbage; toss to coat. Cover and let stand 30 minutes. Toss cabbage mixture well; cover and let stand 30 minutes longer. Drain cabbage. Can be made 8 hours ahead. Cover and chill.

Transfer drained cabbage to another large bowl. Add carrots, green onions, and mayonnaise; toss to coat. Season to taste with salt and pepper.

Yield: 8-10 servings

Jim 'N Nick's
Five Points South • 1908 11th Avenue South • Phone: 205.320.1060
Homewood • 220 Oxmoor Road • Phone: 205.942.3336
Riverchase • 1810 Montgomery Highway • Phone: 205.733.1300
Many other locations: jimnnicks.com

Chopped Salad
Maki Fresh

Maki Creamy Ginger Dressing
2-inch piece fresh ginger
2 garlic cloves
¼ cup chopped shallots
3 tablespoons soy sauce
2 tablespoons granulated sugar
4 cups mayonnaise
3 tablespoons rice wine vinegar
½ teaspoon Sriracha sauce (find in
    Asian or hot sauce aisle)

4 (6-ounce) boneless chicken breasts
Kosher salt
Cracked black pepper
2 tablespoons grapeseed or canola oil
8 cups romaine lettuce (about 2 heads)
1½ cups shredded Napa cabbage
1 cup shelled edamame
1 cup diced English cucumber
1 cup julienne-sliced carrot
1 cup halved grape tomatoes
1 cup Maki Creamy Ginger Dressing
1½ cups cellophane noodles (can substitute
    store-bought wontons)
4 tablespoons toasted sesame seeds

Directions:

For the Maki Creamy Ginger Dressing: Pulse ginger, garlic, shallots, soy, and sugar in blender. In a large mixing bowl, combine mayonnaise, vinegar, Sriracha sauce, and ginger mixture and whisk until thoroughly combined. Store in airtight container and refrigerate.

Preheat grill 400°F.

Coat chicken with oil and season with salt and pepper to taste. Grill chicken about 4 minutes on each side or until an internal temperature of 165°F is reached. Allow chicken to rest for up to 8 minutes so juices redistribute. Cut into bite-size pieces.

Make sure lettuce and cabbage have been washed and dried properly. Cut romaine into bite-size pieces, about one inch. In a large mixing bowl, add lettuce, cabbage, edamame, cucumber, carrot, tomato, and chicken. Toss with ginger dressing. Transfer to your favorite serving piece. Garnish with noodles and sesame seeds.

Yield: 4-6 servings

Maki Fresh
Cahaba Village • 2800 Cahaba Village Plaza • Phone: 205.970.3242
Wells Fargo Tower • 420 20th Street North • Phone: 205.458.4040
makifresh.com

Melt Mac 'N Cheese Sandwich
Melt Restaurant & Food Truck

Mac 'n Cheese
4 cups whole milk
½ cup unsalted butter plus 1 tablespoon
½ cup all-purpose flour
1 small red onion, finely diced
1 sprig of thyme
1 cup mozzarella cheese, grated
1 cup sharp cheddar cheese, grated

½ cup Parmesan cheese, grated
Tabasco sauce and salt to taste
1 pound penne pasta, cooked al dente,
  according to package directions

2 slices Texas toast
1 tablespoon unsalted butter
2 slices American cheese

Directions:
Butter a 3-quart casserole or baking dish with 1 tablespoon butter; set aside. Cook the pasta according to package directions until al dente. Drain well and set aside.

Put the milk and thyme sprig in saucepan over low heat; bring to simmer, but do not boil. In a large saucepan over low heat, melt the butter with diced red onion. Cook until the onions are softened, about 3 minutes. Whisk in the flour, mixing thoroughly, and increase heat, whisking until it reaches a blondish brown color, about 3 minutes. Whisk in the hot milk, adding a little at a time until the mixture is smooth. Cook for 2-3 more minutes over low heat until the mixture thickens and reaches a smooth texture. Strain the mixture to remove the onion and thyme. Return to the pan and add the cheeses, stirring until melted. Add salt and Tabasco sauce to taste.

Add the cooked pasta. Turn the mixture into the prepared dish.

Bake at 425°F until golden brown.

For each sandwich, butter and grill 2 pieces of Texas toast topped with American cheese. When the toast is golden brown, remove it from the grill, top it with a scoop of the Mac 'N Cheese, and it is ready to serve.

Yield: 3 quarts of Mac 'N Cheese (will make a dozen or so sandwiches, depending on the portion size)

Melt
4105 4th Avenue South • Birmingham, Alabama 35222
Phone: 205.917.5000 • meltbham.com
Food Truck Phone: 205.948.3877

P Jack's Fresh Egg Sandwich

Primeaux Cheese & Vino

Sandwich

2 slices sourdough bread, toasted
2 farm-fresh eggs, cooked over medium
4 drops truffle oil
1 pinch sea salt
3 slices Applewood smoked bacon
1 slice Gruyere cheese
2 leaves Owl Hollow Bibb lettuce (or your
   favorite variety)
2 slices tomato

Truffle Aioli

2 eggs
2 cloves garlic, minced
1 teaspoon Dijon mustard
1 lemon, juiced
4 drops Tabasco
4 drops truffle oil
1 ounce Crystal hot sauce
2 cups salad oil
½ teaspoon kosher salt
1 pinch black pepper

Directions:

For the Truffle Aioli: Place eggs, Dijon mustard, garlic, lemon juice, Crystal hot sauce, truffle oil, and Tabasco sauce in food processor, and pulse several times to combine. Turn the processor on run and slowly start streaming in the oil through the tube to make an emulsion. Add salt & pepper. Yield: 2 cups

For the sandwich: Toast the sourdough bread. Cook bacon until crispy and drain off fat. Cook eggs over medium. Place the Bibb lettuce, sliced tomato, bacon, Gruyere cheese, over medium eggs, and 1 pinch sea salt over eggs. Drizzle with truffle oil; then place dollop of truffle aioli on top. Top sandwich with slice of toasted sourdough; cut sandwich in half and serve.

Yield: 1 sandwich

Pesto Chicken Salad
Crestwood Café

Chicken

2 pounds boneless skinless chicken
    breasts, cut into strips
2 quarts water
3 celery stalks, cut into 1-inch lengths
1 cup white onion, coarsely chopped
1 carrot, coarsely chopped
4 sprigs fresh thyme
1 small bunch fresh basil, torn
1 clove garlic
Fresh ground black pepper
1 teaspoon kosher salt

Pesto

2 cups packed fresh basil leaves
2 cloves garlic
⅔ cup extra-virgin olive oil, divided
Kosher salt and freshly ground
    black pepper, to taste
½ cup freshly grated Parmesan cheese

Pesto

2 cups packed fresh basil leaves
2 cloves garlic
⅔ cup extra-virgin olive oil, divided
Kosher salt and freshly ground
    black pepper, to taste
½ cup freshly grated Parmesan cheese

Chicken (cooked and cooled per
    instructions), cut into ¼-inch pieces
    (substitute rotisserie chicken if desired)
⅓ cup red onion, finely diced
⅓ cup celery, finely diced
⅛ cup pecans, chopped
1 tablespoon Mrs. Dash seasoning (find in
    the spice aisle)
1 tablespoon lemon pepper
1 cup mayonnaise
½ cup Dijon mustard
½ cup pesto, or more as desired

Directions:

Cook the Chicken: Combine all ingredients in a stock pot and cook until internal temperature of the chicken reaches 165°F. Remove chicken from the water and place in refrigerator to cool. Drain liquid from vegetables, and reserve stock for your next soup.

Make the Pesto: Combine the basil and garlic in a food processor and pulse until coarsely chopped. Add ½ cup of the oil and process until fully incorporated and smooth. Season with salt and pepper. Add all the remaining oil and pulse until smooth. Transfer the pesto to another bowl and mix in the cheese. Makes 2 cups.

Assemble the chicken salad: In a large serving bowl, combine all ingredients, including the pesto, until well combined. Serve salad on a bed of lettuce, on bread as a sandwich, or with crackers.

Yield: 2 pounds chicken salad

Crestwood Café
5512 Crestwood Boulevard • Birmingham, Alabama 35212
Phone: 205.595.0300 • crestwoodcafe.com

Pimento Cheese Sliders

Rogue Tavern

Pimento Cheese
1 pound shredded cheddar cheese
2 red bell peppers, grilled, peeled, and
    diced small
8 ounces cream cheese
¼ cup mayonnaise
1 tablespoon Tabasco® sauce
¼ cup Sriracha® sauce
1 tablespoon salt
1 tablespoon pepper

*Prepare the pimento cheese ahead of
time and refrigerate. See directions below.

Beef Sliders
2 pounds ground beef
Salt
Pepper
Garlic
8 slices bacon, cooked and sliced in
    half, horizontally
2 tomatoes, sliced thin
8 slider buns, toasted if you prefer

Directions:
For the Pimento Cheese: Grill the red peppers on high heat for 20 minutes, turning often until very soft. Remove from the grill. Put them in a bowl and cover with plastic wrap. Let peppers cool. Peel the skin off the grilled pepper and slice in half. Remove the veins and seeds. Dice the peppers very small. Combine the other ingredients in a large bowl and mix together well. Refrigerate until needed. Yield: 1 pound pimento cheese spread.

For the Beef Sliders: Mix the ground beef in a bowl and season to taste with salt, pepper, and garlic. Divide the ground beef into 8 equal portions. Make patties thinner in the middle and thicker on the outside edges for best results. Grill to your desired temperature on a grill or indoor grill pan. (Medium is 145°F)

While the burgers are on the grill, cook the bacon, and cut in half. Slice the tomatoes. Toast the buns, if you desire.

To assemble the sliders: To each bun add 1 burger patty, a slice of tomato, a heaping spoonful of pimento cheese, and top it with 2 pieces of bacon.

Yield: 8 sliders

Rogue Tavern
2312 2nd Avenue North • Birmingham, Alabama 35203
Phone: 205.202.4151 • roguetavern.com

The Red, White and Blue Burger

On Tap Sports Café

2¼ pounds Black Angus ground beef
⅓ cup roasted red bell peppers, diced (Roast
    or purchase them in the condiment aisle.)
1 teaspoon minced garlic
1 teaspoon ground black pepper
3 teaspoons Worcestershire sauce
6 ounces cream cheese, softened
⅓ cup sun-dried tomatoes, finely chopped
3 ounces blue cheese, softened
1 teaspoon hot chili sauce or Tabasco sauce

6 slices red onions
12 lettuce leaves
12 slices of tomato
½ cup chives
6 pretzel buns

Hot Sauce and Ranch Blend
¼ cup of your favorite hot sauce
1 cup ranch dressing (make or purchase)

Directions:

Make the burger: Blend ground beef with garlic, black pepper, and diced red peppers with a splash of Worcestershire sauce. Form into a ball. Divide into 6 portions. Shape into patties. Set aside.

For the special cheese blend: Blend the cream cheese, blue cheese, sun-dried tomatoes, and a splash of hot chili sauce together. Set aside.

For the Hot Sauce and Ranch Blend: Mix ¼ cup hot sauce with 1 cup ranch dressing. Set aside.

Grill burgers until medium or to your preference, approximately 8-10 minutes. Medium is 140°F. Add a heaping tablespoon of special cheese blend on top of each burger patty. Cover with a heatproof lid to help the melting process. Once melted, remove from heat and allow to rest for a few minutes.

Butter the pretzel buns. Toast lightly. Dress the burger with lettuce, tomato, red onion slices, and chives. Drizzle with hot sauce and ranch blend.

Yield: 6 burgers

On Tap Sports Café
Fultondale • 1600 Main Street • Phone: 205.745.4888
Galleria • 3440 Galleria Circle • Phone: 205.988.3203
Inverness • 810 Inverness Corners • Phone: 205.437.1999
Lakeview • 737 29th Street South • Phone: 320.1225
ontapsportscafe.com

Lower Alabama Seafood Gumbo
Baumhower's Restaurant

1½ cups vegetable oil
1½ cups flour
4 cups diced onion
2 cups diced celery
1 cup diced bell pepper
½ cup minced garlic
3 pounds gumbo crabs, cut in half (find in the freezer section)
1½ gallons water
2½ pounds shrimp (51/60 count, fresh or frozen)
1½ pounds okra
1 cup diced tomato
4 bay leaves

1 pound claw crabmeat
¼ cup Baumhower's hot sauce
3 tablespoons Maggi Seasoning (available in some grocery stores in the Latin or Asian aisle)
½ cup Worcestershire sauce
¼ cup lime juice
1 tablespoon Creole seasoning (such as Tony Chachere's)
1 tablespoon black pepper
2 teaspoons white pepper
½ teaspoon red pepper
½ gallon oysters
2½ pounds catfish, cut into cubes

Directions:

Heat oil until it sizzles when you sprinkle in a little flour. Add flour and stir constantly until you have a dark roux.

Add onions, celery, bell pepper, garlic, and gumbo crabs in the oil. Sauté together until celery and onion have turned translucent. Add water while whisking to incorporate roux. Add ½ pound shrimp, okra, tomato, and bay leaves, and bring mixture to a temperature of 195°F.

Add all other ingredients except 2 pounds shrimp, oysters and catfish. Lightly simmer 90 minutes, skimming oil and froth from perimeter of the pot.

Add remaining shrimp, cubed catfish, and oysters. Cook 15 minutes until shrimp are cooked through. Serve or chill the pot down quickly in an ice bath if serving at a later date. (Gumbo is always better the second day after all the flavors have a chance to blend together.)

Be sure to check for crab shells if any of them have broken during cooking.

Yield: 3 gallons

Baumhower's Restaurant
Lee Branch • 1001 Doug Baker Boulevard #112, Birmingham • Phone: 205.995.5151
Patton Creek • 4445 Creekside Avenue, Hoover • Phone: 205.403.7474
And many other locations • baumhowers.com

BAUMHOWER'S
HOT SAUCE

Sliced Tomatoes with Marinated Gulf Crabmeat, Cucumbers, and Cider Vinegar

Highlands Bar and Grill · Chef Frank Stitt

James Beard Foundation Award Winner

4 Cherokee Purple or Black Krim tomatoes

2 medium to small Green Zebra tomatoes (optional)

2 medium to small yellow tomatoes (optional)

12 golden cherry tomatoes, such as Sun Gold or Golden Nugget, cut into quarters

8 red cherry tomatoes, such as Super Sweet 100, cut into quarters

1 shallot, finely minced

3 ounces apple cider honey vinegar

Kosher or sea salt

9 ounces mild, fruity extra virgin olive oil

2 small, firm cucumbers, half skin peeled like a zebra, seeds removed if they have formed. Ideally, choose the small cucumbers whose seeds have not matured. Cut into half-moons, about ⅛ inch thick. Place in a small bowl, season with a pinch of salt, and place in refrigerator for 10 minutes or longer.

1 pound jumbo lump crabmeat, picked free of all shell (You will need about 12 ounces for this recipe; save remainder for the following day or serve a huge portion.)

4 large basil leaves, finely chopped

4 mint leaves, finely chopped

A few fresh chives, finely chopped

Freshly ground Tellicherry black peppercorns

Directions:

Trim the tomatoes and remove a tiny slice from the bottoms. Trim away the top cores and any underripe shoulders. Slice into thick, even slices. Remember that tomatoes are better if never refrigerated.

In a medium mixing bowl, add the shallot, vinegar, salt, and pepper and allow to macerate for 10-15 minutes. Whisk in the olive oil.

Place the crabmeat in a mixing bowl and add the herbs, 3 tablespoons of the reserved vinaigrette, and a little salt and freshly ground black pepper. Toss delicately to combine.

Season the tomatoes with salt and pepper, place in a large shallow bowl, and add 3 tablespoons of vinaigrette. Carefully coat with dressing.

Highlands Bar and Grill
2011 11th Avenue South • Birmingham, Alabama 35205
Phone: 205.939.1400 • highlandsbarandgrill.com

Arrange on plates, scattering the cherry tomatoes around; add the cucumbers, and place the crabmeat in the center. Drizzle with a little more vinaigrette and serve.

Chef's Note: A Provençal Rosé or an Austrian Riesling or Grüner should go nicely.

Yield: 4 servings

Smoked Trout Salad with Fennel and Champagne Shallots

Bottle & Bone

1 fennel bulb, trimmed
2 shallots, thinly sliced
2 cloves garlic, minced
¼ cup Champagne
2 tablespoons apple cider vinegar
½ cup créme fraîche (store bought or you can make your own)
¼ cup extra-virgin olive oil
2 tablespoons freshly grated lemon zest
2 tablespoons togarashi (a Japanese pepper spice, found at well-stocked grocery stores or
    Asian markets)
1 tablespoon fresh horseradish
3-4 cups smoked trout, picked over and flaked into chunks
2 tablespoons flat-leaf parsley, chopped
Salt and pepper to taste

Directions:

Cut fennel bulb into thin slices. Save the green tops and chop them. Combine sliced fennel, chopped fennel tops, shallots, garlic, Champagne, and vinegar. Place in a saucepan over medium heat and bring to a boil. Remove from heat. Strain the liquid into a heatproof bowl, and put the strained vegetables into another bowl. Let both completely cool.

Add créme fraîche, olive oil, lemon zest, togarashi, and horseradish to the liquid and whisk until blended. Add cooked vegetables and toss.

Add trout to cooked vegetables and fold gently, coating each flake of trout and vegetables. Add parsley, and season to taste.

Serve on top of a plate of arugula, or just eat the salad with bread of choice. The lemons used for zest can also be squeezed over the salad for another hint of freshness.

Yield: 4 servings

Bottle & Bone
2311 Richard Arrington Jr. Boulevard, North Suite #200 • Birmingham, Alabama 35203
Phone: 205.538.7106 • bottleandbone.com

The James Beard Burger

V. Richard's Market

2 pounds fresh ground chuck
1 red onion, finely grated
1 ounce heavy cream
Salt and pepper to taste
4 sesame seed buns (Ours are housemade.)
Butter or oil
Cheese, optional
Spring mix
2 tomatoes, thinly sliced
Red onion, thinly sliced
Pickle spear

Directions:

In a bowl, finely grate the onion and add it to the meat. Add heavy cream and mix it all together, taking care not to overwork the meat. Just combine it well enough to blend together. Separate the mixture into 4 equal parts. Add salt and pepper to your own taste. Shape into patties. Cook burgers on medium-high heat (Do not mash.) for 6 minutes on each side for a medium (140°F) burger. Set aside to rest.

Next, spread a small amount of butter or oil on the bun and toast. If you are adding cheese, this is the perfect time to add it to the bun. The reason we add the cheese to the bun is because our housemade bread soaks up all of the wonderful juice in the burger and sometimes it may fall apart. To keep the burger intact we add the cheese to the bun to create a nice coating and that way it melts into the burger once assembled.

Once your bun is done, place on dish, add the burger patty and lettuce, onion, and tomato. Serve with condiments of your choice and a pickle spear.

Yield: 4 burgers

V. Richards Market
V. Richards has since closed, but you can still make this neighborhood favorite burger!
vrichards.net

The Knuckle Sandwich
Sautéed Lobster with Tarragon Mayo, Marinated Tomatoes, and Grilled Scallion on Focaccia

Oscar's at the Museum

3 Roma tomatoes
1 bunch fresh tarragon, reserve 1 teaspoon
1 tablespoon red wine vinegar
1½ tablespoons olive oil, plus a bit to drizzle
½ teaspoon turmeric
Salt and pepper
¼ cup Duke's mayonnaise

3½ ounces lobster meat
1-2 tablespoons unsalted butter
2 scallions, ends trimmed
2 slices red onion, sliced very thinly
¼ cup Parmesan-Reggiano, grated
Focaccia bread sliced in half, sandwich size
Mixed greens

Directions:
Preheat oven to 400°F.

For the Marinated Tomatoes: Dice only 2 of the tomatoes; reserve the other one for later. Add 1 teaspoon finely chopped tarragon, red wine vinegar, olive oil, turmeric, salt, and pepper to taste. Mix together in a bowl and set aside.

For the Tarragon Mayonnaise: Add remaining tarragon, mayonnaise, and salt to food processor and process until smooth. Check seasoning. Add more salt if necessary. Set aside.

Sauté the lobster in a little butter; season with salt and pepper. Set aside.

Grill scallions on a grill pan or on a grill until soft and slightly charred.

For the Lid: Thinly slice the remaining tomato. Top the sandwich lid in this order: sliced tomato, red onions, and grated Parmesan, drizzled with a little olive oil. Bake at 400°F until cheese is melted and bread is toasted.

Assemble the sandwich: Butter the bottom of the Focaccia and toast on grill pan, toaster oven, or in the oven. Remove. Spread both sides of the bread with tarragon mayonnaise. Place the lobster meat on the bottom slice of bread; top with the mixed greens, marinated tomatoes, and the grilled scallion. Top with baked lid. Slice in half.

Yield: 1 sandwich

Oscar's at the Museum
2000 Reverend Abraham Woods, Jr. Boulevard • Birmingham, Alabama 35203
Phone: 205.254.2565 • artsbma.org/visit/oscars/

Tomato Bisque with Ginger Ranch Cream
Silvertron Café

1 carrot, finely diced
1 medium white onion, finely diced
1 stalk of celery, finely diced
1 teaspoon olive oil
Pinch salt and pepper
⅔ cup butter (1 stick plus 2½ tablespoons)
¾ cup all-purpose flour
1 quart milk
2 (14-ounce) cans tomato juice
Salt and pepper to taste
Cayenne pepper (optional)

Ginger Ranch Cream
2 teaspoons freshly grated ginger
1 cup ranch dressing (homemade or store-bought)

Directions:
Add the carrot, onion, and celery to a large stock pot over medium heat; add olive oil and a pinch of salt and pepper; sauté vegetables until soft.

Once vegetables are soft, add the butter. Once the butter is melted but not browned, add the flour and stir until thick, and you have cooked the raw taste from the flour, about 3-4 minutes. Next, very slowly whisk in ½ cup milk; then, once it is incorporated, slowly whisk in the remaining milk, whisking constantly.

After the milk is fully incorporated, add the tomato juice and simmer over medium heat for 30 minutes. Use an immersion blender to puree the vegetables until smooth, or you may strain out the vegetables, puree them in a blender, and then return them to the soup.

Adjust the salt and pepper to taste. Add a touch of cayenne if desired.

For the Ginger Ranch Cream: Grate fresh ginger into ranch dressing and process in blender. Spoon a dollop of cream onto soup before serving.

Yield: 2 quarts

Silvertron Café
3813 Clairmont Avenue • Birmingham, Alabama 35222
Phone: 205.591.3707 • silvertroncafe.us

Grass-Fed Beef Willis Burger
Shindigs Catering & Food Truck

16 ounces local, grass-fed ground beef
    portioned into 4 (4-ounce) balls
4 tablespoons Special Sauce
2½ tablespoons Fig Mostarda
2 tablespoons Truffle Yogurt
2 slices Applewood bacon, cooked crispy
1½ ounces Bleu Cheese
5 tablespoons Roasted Garlic Butter
¼ cup organic arugula
1½ teaspoons lemon oil
1½ teaspoons salt
1 bun

Special Sauce
1 cup Worcestershire sauce
½ cup balsamic vinegar
1 fresh bay leaf (laurel)
1 Morita chili, crushed
4 sprigs fresh thyme
1 tablespoon black peppercorns
1½ teaspoons onion powder
1½ teaspoons garlic powder

Roasted Garlic Butter
2 heads garlic, reserve 2 cloves for the
    Truffle Yogurt
2 sticks unsalted butter
2 cups extra virgin olive oil

Fig Mostarda
2 large Vidalia onions, julienned
2 quarts local figs, trimmed
½ cup red wine
½ cup Acai juice (or Blueberry POM)
2 cups balsamic vinegar
1 cup sorghum syrup
1 teaspoon vanilla bean paste (available at
    most cooking supply stores)
3 tablespoons Chinese mustard powder
    (available at most Asian markets)
2 tablespoons fresh thyme

Truffle Yogurt
1 cup Greek yogurt
1 tablespoon of Roasted Garlic Butter
¼ teaspoon fresh ground black pepper
¼ teaspoon fresh lemon juice
¼ teaspoon truffle salt (available at
    kitchen/cook supply stores)
½ teaspoon white truffle oil (available at
    kitchen/cook supply stores)
1 tablespoon Fines-Herbes, chopped (Typically
    fresh parsley, tarragon, chives, chervil
    are used.)

Directions:

For the Special Sauce: Put everything in a pot. Steep for 30 minutes. Strain into a glass jar and set aside.

For the Roasted Garlic Butter: Put everything in a pot. Bring to a boil; lower heat to simmer for 30 minutes. Strain into a glass jar and set aside. Yield: 1 cup.

Shindigs Catering & Food Truck
Business: 205.538.1170 • Order Line: 205.807.0299
shindigscateringtrucks.com

For the Fig Mostarda: Trim figs and onions. Add 2 tablespoons of garlic butter to a large pot or saucepan. Cook until caramelized; then add thyme. Deglaze with the red wine, Acai juice, and balsamic vinegar. Add sorghum and vanilla extract; then let simmer for 30 minutes to reduce. Make a slurry by combining the mustard powder and hot water to make paste. Add after the 30 minutes to thicken the Mostarda. Pour into a food processor. Pulse until slightly chunky, but spreadable. Set aside.

For the Truffle Yogurt: Combine ingredients and set aside.

To assemble: Brush the insides of the top and bottom of each bun with the garlic butter. Toast on a griddle or hot, cast iron skillet. Smear the bun top with the Fig Mostarda. Smear the bottom bun with the Truffle Yogurt. Season arugula with salt, pepper, and the lemon oil, and place on top and bottom buns. Season the beef; then place the 4 (4-ounce) balls of beef on the very hot griddle and press thin right away with a very hot grill press to flatten. Cook until caramelized, about 1-1½ minutes. Flip and immediately baste with the Special Sauce. Working speedily, top one patty with your favorite Bleu Cheese and the slice of bacon. Rapidly repeat with the other patty. Stack the patties together and place on the bottom bun. Finally, place other bun on top and proceed to eat.

Yield: 4 extra-deluxe burgers

The Main Course

"Vitello Tonnato" with a Bit of Pig Seared Yellowfin Tuna, Bacon Wrapped Veal Sweetbreads, and Lemon Picatta Sauce

Grace Revival · Chef/Owner Haller Magee

8 ounces sushi grade tuna
1 pound veal sweetbreads (Ask your
   butcher for heart lobes.)
8 thin slices of Applewood smoked bacon
1 cup capers, rinsed and drained
2 shallots, finely diced
6 garlic cloves, finely minced
Juice of 2 lemons

¼ cup white wine
¼ cup chicken stock
¼ cup canola oil
¼ pound unsalted butter
2 tablespoons chopped parsley
2 tablespoons chopped chives
Salt and pepper to taste

Directions:

For the Veal Sweetbreads: Soak in water to cover for at least 6 hours, changing water every few hours. Drain sweetbreads. Fill a large pot with lightly salted water and bring to a boil. Add sweetbreads and simmer for 2-3 minutes. Drain and place in an ice water bath to cool. Then drain and place them on a towel-lined baking sheet and cover with another towel, another baking sheet, and a light weight. The sweetbreads should compress, but not be severely flattened. Refrigerate overnight.

To complete: Preheat the oven to 350°F. Remove sweetbreads from refrigerator, remove sinew from sweetbreads, and cut them into 4 individual pieces. Wrap each with 2 slices of bacon that meet with the seam. Season tuna and sweetbreads with salt and pepper. Heat 2 large sauté pans until very hot, and add a tablespoon of canola oil to each. In one pan, place tuna and cook on each side for 1½ minutes to sear. Remove tuna and let rest. Reserve pan tuna was cooked in. Place bacon-wrapped sweetbreads in the other pan and cook, seam side down, for 2-3 minutes. Now turn sweetbreads over, mount 1 tablespoon of butter in pan, and place in oven for 3 more minutes. Now, reheat the pan the tuna was cooked in, to build the sauce. Add a bit more oil, shallots, garlic, and capers. Sweat vegetables for a minute or so, and deglaze with white wine.

Reminder: Don't forget to pull the sweetbreads out of the oven and let rest. Wait a minute, and add stock and lemon juice. Let this cook together for 2 minutes or until liquid is halfway reduced. Now pull sauce off heat and add parsley, chives, and a heaping tablespoon of butter. Stir the sauce to incorporate ingredients.

Grace Revival
Chef Haller Magee's restaurant is not open but please enjoy his recipe.

To Plate: Slice the tuna into 8 slices. The tuna should still be a nice medium rare. Assemble in the center of four plates. Spoon a bit of the sauce around the tuna and just a bit on top. Place sweetbreads on top of the tuna. Spoon a bit more sauce on top of the sweetbreads.

Yield: 4 servings

Bob's Authentic BarB-Q Tacos

Bob Sykes BarB-Q, Bessemer

Homemade Tortillas
2 cups Maseca instant corn flour
2 cups warm water
Plastic wax paper

Tacos
4 cups shredded barbecue pork or chicken
1 tomato, chopped
½ onion, chopped
2 ounces lemon juice

1 bunch of cilantro, chopped
Salt to taste
Black pepper to taste
1 whole jalapeno (optional)
4 cups shredded barbecue pork or chicken
Shredded cheddar cheese
Shredded lettuce
Salsa (store bought)
Lime wedges, optional

Directions:
Preheat the grill pan or griddle to 400°F.

For the Homemade Tortillas: Combine Maseca and water. Knead 4 minutes. Roll into 16 small balls. Put each ball on a tortilla press between 2 pieces of plastic wax paper. Press down to make into thin tortillas (approximately 16 inches in diameter). If you do not have a tortilla press, you can use the bottom of a large, heavy cast iron skillet or heavy pan to help press the tortillas out even and flat.

Place tortilla on a pre-heated flat grill or use a large grill pan or cast iron skillet if you do not have a flat grill. When the edges curl up, flip the tortilla. When the tortilla puffs slightly, it is done.

For the Tacos: Mix tomato, onion, lemon juice, cilantro, salt, and pepper, along with jalapeno, if desired. Place about ¼ cup barbecue pork or chicken into each taco. Sprinkle cheese and lettuce over meat, and top with salsa.

Serve with lime wedges.

Yield: 16 tacos

Z's Baked Chicken and Fresh Collard Greens

Z's Restaurant · Chef Gregory Peoples

Baked Chicken

1 whole chicken

2 tablespoons Lawry's Chicken and
    Poultry Rub

2 tablespoons paprika

2 tablespoons onion powder

2 tablespoons granulated garlic or
    garlic powder

Collard Greens

1 head of collards

4 cups low-sodium chicken broth

¼ cup extra virgin olive oil

1 large yellow onion, sliced

1 tablespoon white distilled vinegar

1 teaspoon garlic powder

1 teaspoon onion powder

1 teaspoon black pepper

1 teaspoon white granulated sugar

1 teaspoon salt

½ stick unsalted butter

1 teaspoon white distilled vinegar

*Season to taste. Add more seasoning
    if desired.

Directions:

For the Baked Chicken: Preheat oven to 350°F. Rinse the chicken and pat dry with paper towels. Cut up chicken into 8 pieces or you can ask to have the chicken cut up for you at the market. Put chicken into a plastic bowl along with the remaining ingredients. Cover the bowl with plastic wrap and place bowl in refrigerator. Let chicken marinate for 30 minutes -1 hour.

Fill shallow baking pan ¼ the way full with water. Place the chicken in the pan; wrap with aluminum foil and place in the oven. Cook 45 minutes to an hour or until internal temperature of chicken reaches 165°F with an instant thermometer. Remove the foil and let chicken brown until color meets your satisfaction. (No more than 10-15 minutes.) Remove the pan from oven, and let the chicken rest for 5-7 minutes to seal in the juices before serving.

Yield: 4 servings

For the Collard Greens: Wash collards, dry, and remove stems running down the center of each leaf. Place 3-4 leaves at a time on top of each other. Roll them like you would a cigar or sushi roll. Cut the roll, horizontally, into ⅛ or ¼ size ribbons. Put broth in a 4-quart pot and put on medium-to-high heat. Add seasonings, 1 tablespoon vinegar, and collards to broth. Let cook for about 45 minutes; then check to see if they are done. Once done, add half-a-stick of unsalted butter to reintroduce fat. (Butter will help with tenderness.) Add 1 teaspoon white distilled vinegar to taste.

Yield: 4 servings

Real Black Angus Beef Brisket
Full Moon Bar-B-Que

½ cup garlic salt
½ cup kosher salt
½ cup black pepper
½ cup dried oregano
½ cup onion powder
½ cup Lawry's Seasoning (found in the spice aisle)
1 (5-pound) certified Black Angus brisket
Vegetable oil

Directions:
Start by making sure to purchase real, certified Black Angus brisket. Typical size is around 5 pounds.

In a bowl, combine all the dry ingredients in equal parts, making sure there is enough to liberally coat the brisket.

Lightly rub the brisket with oil. Coat the brisket with the dry rub, making sure the entire brisket is covered and packed with the rub.

Place the brisket in the smoker, uncovered, with the fat cap facing up, so that the fat drips down onto the meat.

Smoke 4-6 hours or until the internal temperature is 165°F. Make sure to let the meat rest for about 30 minutes before slicing.

Yield: based on portion sizes

Full Moon Bar-B-Que
The Original/Southside • 525 25th Street South • Phone: 205.324.1007
Hoover • 2000 Patton Chapel Road • Phone: 205.822.6666
Inverness • 4635 US Highway 280 • Phone: 205.991.7328
Valley Avenue • 337 Valley Avenue • Phone: 205.945.9997
For additional locations and information: fullmoonbbq.com

Braised Lamb Shanks with Carrots and Pearl Onions

Vino

4 lamb shanks, thawed if frozen
1 cup all-purpose flour
1 teaspoon salt
1 teaspoon black pepper
1 cup onions, chopped
1 cup celery, chopped
1 pound "fat" small carrots, cut in half
1 heaping tablespoon garlic, chopped
1 cup beef broth
1 cup chicken broth
Scant pinch ground cinnamon
4 pearl onions, whole
4 garlic cloves, whole
1 sprig rosemary (remove the stems after cooking)
Enough chicken broth to cover shanks, approximately 1 (32-ounce) carton, depending on the
    size of the pot

Directions:
Make a seasoned flour by combining the flour, salt, and pepper in a shallow bowl or pan.
Dredge the shanks in the seasoned flour, making sure to lightly coat all sides. In a Dutch oven
on medium heat, add a turn of olive oil to the pan and heat until it shimmers. Once it is hot,
add the shanks and brown on all sides, allowing time for a light crust to form before you turn
it. Remove the shanks and lightly sauté the chopped onions and celery. Add the chopped garlic
and lightly toss together. Add 1 cup each beef and chicken broth, along with the cinnamon,
and bring to a boil. Return the lamb to the Dutch oven and add the pearl onions, garlic cloves,
and rosemary. Top off with enough chicken broth to cover the shanks. Put the top on the Dutch
oven and bake at 350°F for approximately 4 hours or until tender, adding carrots after 2 hours
of baking time.

Yield: 4 servings

Vino
1930 Cahaba Road, English Village • Mountain Brook, Alabama 35223
Phone: 205.870.8404 • vinobirmingham.com

Cajun Ahi Tuna with Thai Mango Jicama Salad

Century Restaurant & Bar, The Tutwiler Hotel

Cajun Spice Rub
10 tablespoons blackened seasoning
5 teaspoons cayenne pepper
5 teaspoons chili powder
5 teaspoons ground cumin
5 teaspoons curry powder
5 teaspoons of ground cinnamon
5 teaspoons paprika

Mango Thai Jicama Salad
1 mango
1 cup jicama
1 red bell pepper
½ red onion
8 sprigs of cilantro
½ teaspoon Thai curry paste
1 ounce rice wine vinegar
1 tablespoon honey
1 tablespoon lime juice
1 tablespoon olive oil
4 (6-ounce) portions Ahi tuna

Directions:

To prepare Cajun Spice Rub: Combine blackened seasoning and next 6 ingredients. Mix all spices together until fully incorporated.

To prepare Mango Thai Jicama Salad: Peel, pit, and slice mango into thin strips. Peel and slice jicama into thin strips. Seed red bell pepper and slice into thin strips. Peel and slice red onion. In mixing bowl, combine mango, jicama, bell pepper, onion, cilantro, curry paste, vinegar, honey, and lime juice, stirring well. Set aside.

Roll each piece of tuna in Cajun Seasoning until fully encrusted. Set aside.

Add 1 tablespoon olive oil to a hot sauté pan; sear tuna until golden brown on all sides, about 10-15 seconds on each side.

Place ¼ of mango salad in the center of each plate. Thinly slice tuna and fan around the top of the salad.

Yield: 4 servings

Century Restaurant & Bar, The Tutwiler Hotel
2021 Park Place • Birmingham, Alabama 35203
Phone: 205.458.9707 • centurybirmingham.com

Filet Fricassee
Bellinis Ristorante

4 ears summer corn
½ teaspoon salt
¼ teaspoon pepper
1 pound fingerling potatoes
½ teaspoon salt
¼ teaspoon pepper
¼ cup olive oil, divided
1 bunch Vidalia onions, sliced
4 (6-8-ounce) beef tenderloin steaks

1 teaspoon salt
½ teaspoon pepper
2 tablespoons olive oil
1 bunch fresh basil, thinly sliced
¼ teaspoon salt
⅛ teaspoon pepper
8 ounces Gorgonzola cheese
Balsamic glaze (can be purchased)

Directions:
Preheat oven to 400°F.

Boil ears of corn 3-4 minutes or until tender. Drain. Season corn with salt and pepper and grill for just a few minutes to caramelize kernels. Let cool. Cut kernels from corn, and set aside.

Slice potatoes in half lengthwise and boil with salt 4-6 minutes or until al dente. Toss potatoes with salt, pepper, 2 tablespoons olive oil, and sliced Vidalia onion. Roast in a 400°F oven 10-15 minutes or until brown and crispy.

Season steaks with salt and pepper and grill to desired temperature. Set aside to rest.

Heat remaining 2 tablespoons olive oil in a sauté pan. Add corn, basil, salt, and pepper and cook 1 minute or until thoroughly heated. Turn off heat and add cheese.

Slice steaks in half to make 2 circles. Spoon corn mixture onto plate and top with 1 filet round. Next, layer potatoes, then the other slice of filet. Finish with more of the corn mixture and drizzle with balsamic glaze.

Yield: 4 servings

Bellinis Ristorante
6801 Cahaba Valley Road • Birmingham, Alabama 35242
Phone: 205.981.5380 • ourbellinis.supportlocalflavor.com

Garlic Citrus Shrimp with Grilled Hearts of Palm
Copper Pot Kitchen

20-30 large shrimp, peeled and deveined
¼ cup extra virgin olive oil + 3 tablespoons
2 oranges, zest and juice
2 limes, zest and juice
5 cloves of garlic, sliced
3 cans hearts of palm or where available (24 ounces fresh hearts of palm)
4 teaspoons sea salt
2 teaspoons white pepper

Directions:

Peel and devein the shrimp. Julienne the hearts of palm. Toss the hearts of palm with 3 tablespoons olive oil, 2 teaspoons salt and 1 teaspoon pepper and half of the orange and lime zest and juice. Grill over low heat using a non-stick grill pan.

In a sauté pan, heat the olive oil over a medium flame. Add the sliced garlic and sauté until the garlic begins to take on color. Season the shrimp with the remaining salt and pepper and cook for 2-3 minutes. Add the remaining orange and lime juice and zest. Sauté the shrimp for 2-3 minutes more or until lightly pink. Toss shrimp with grilled hearts of palm and serve.

Yield: 3-4 servings

Note: Copper Pot Kitchen is not a restaurant but is an avid supporter and sponsor of the Birmingham Library's 2014 Eat Drink Read Write Festival.

Copper Pot Kitchen
Birmingham, Alabama
Phone: 205.641.3621 • copperpotkitchen.com

Gigged Apalachicola Flounder with Romano Beans, 'Just Dug' Potatoes, and Sauce Gribiche

Bottega Restaurant · Chef Frank Stitt

James Beard Foundation Award Winner

Sauce Gribiche
1 cup mayonnaise
1 teaspoon Dijon mustard
½ cup Idaho potatoes, boiled and diced
1 tablespoon cornichon, minced
1 tablespoon capers, minced
1 tablespoon chives, chopped
½ tablespoon dill, chopped
2 eggs, hard boiled and chopped
Juice of 1 lemon
Tabasco sauce to taste
Salt and pepper to taste

2 cups fingerling potatoes, 'just dug' if possible
1 cup green beans – such as Blue Lake or Kentucky Wonder, all trimmed
2 tablespoons canola oil
4 (6-ounce) flounder fillets – freshest you can find, such as gigged flounder from
    Apalachicola Bay
Salt
Freshly ground black pepper
1 tablespoon unsalted butter
1 cup green Romano beans
1 cup yellow Romano beans
2 shallots, finely minced

Directions:
For the Sauce Gribiche: In large mixing bowl, combine all ingredients and mix together well. Season with Tabasco sauce, salt, and pepper to taste. Set aside.

Wash and boil potatoes 15 minutes or until just tender. Cut into half lengthwise, and set aside.

Trim and wash beans and blanch in salted water about 3 minutes until just crisp. Shock in ice water and pat dry. Set beans aside.

Bottega Restaurant
2240 Highland Avenue South • Birmingham, Alabama 35205
Phone: 205.939.1000 • bottegarestaurant.com

Pat fish fillets dry and season with salt and pepper. In a pan just large enough to hold all 4 fillets, heat oil over moderately-high heat and, when almost smoking, carefully add fish, skin side up. Adjust heat to moderate and cook until golden – about 4 minutes. Turn and continue cooking until almost done – about another 3 minutes. Remove and place on resting rack and keep warm.

Meanwhile in a large pan, heat butter, and add potatoes, shallots, and beans. Toss over medium heat until slightly crispy – about 3 minutes. Season with salt and pepper and serve with flounder and Sauce Gribiche.

Yield: 4 servings

Grilled Chicken Thigh Paillard with Salsa Verde, Arugula and Frisée

Bottega Café · Chef Frank Stitt

James Beard Foundation Award Winner

4 (5-6-ounce) natural fresh boneless, skinless chicken thighs, pounded to even thickness
2 tablespoons kosher salt

Salsa Verde
½ cup flat-leaf parsley
¼ cup mint
4 tarragon sprigs, leaves only
1 small garlic clove, crushed and finely chopped
1 tablespoon capers

1-2 anchovy filets (optional)
1 teaspoon Dijon mustard
1 tablespoon shallot, finely minced
1 cup olive oil
1 tablespoon champagne vinegar
Kosher salt
Freshly ground black pepper

1 cup arugula
1 cup frisée

Directions:

Season chicken lightly with salt; place it on butcher paper, and refrigerate 12 to 24 hours.

To prepare Salsa Verde: Combine herbs, garlic, one-half of capers, one-half shallot, and olive oil in a food processor. Pulse to achieve a chunky blend.

Transfer to a bowl and fold in remaining capers, mustard, shallot, and vinegar. Season with salt and pepper to taste.

Heat a grill or ridged skillet over moderately high heat.

Drizzle chicken with olive oil and season with black pepper. Grill until lightly charred, about 3 minutes. Turn and cook other side until done, about another 3 minutes.

Serve with a little salad of arugula and frisée, drizzled with Salsa Verde.

Yield: 4 servings

Bottega Café
2240 Highland Avenue South • Birmingham, Alabama 35205
Phone: 205.939.1000 • bottegarestaurant.com/cafe

Gulf Coast Black Grouper, Grilled Chilton County Peaches, Shallot Vinaigrette

Ocean • Chef/Owner George Reis

½ cup mirin* (a sweet Japanese rice wine found in grocery store's Asian aisle)
Juice of 1 lemon
Salt and pepper to taste
4 peaches, cut in half, seeds removed (do not peel peaches)

Shallot Mustard Vinaigrette
1 tablespoon shallots, julienne cut
1 teaspoon extra virgin olive oil plus ⅔ cup
⅓ cup rice wine vinegar (found in most grocery stores in the Asian aisle)

2 teaspoons Dijon mustard
1 teaspoon flat leaf parsley, minced

4 (7 ounce) black grouper fillets (substitute snapper if the grouper is unavailable)
Olive oil
Salt and pepper

Directions:

For the marinade: Blend mirin, lemon juice, salt, and pepper together in a nonreactive bowl. Add peaches and allow all to sit for 15-20 minutes. (*If you cannot find mirin; substitute by using ½ tablespoon granulated sugar dissolved into ½ cup of white wine, vermouth, or dry sherry.)

For the Shallot Mustard Vinaigrette: Sauté shallots in one teaspoon olive oil in a small saucepan until caramelized. Transfer to a large bowl, whisk in rice wine vinegar, mustard, and parsley. Gradually stream in remaining ⅔ cup olive oil, whisking constantly to create an emulsion. Yield: 1 cup

For the Grouper: Preheat the grill to medium-high. (I prefer using a wood or charcoal fire.) Season both sides of the fish with salt and pepper. Brush with olive oil. Place on a well-oiled grill and cook for 5-6 minutes per side or until fish is just cooked through. Meanwhile, on a slightly cooler spot on the grill, add the peaches, flesh side down. Cook for several minutes until well-marked, turn over and cook through.

To serve: Place 2 peach halves on the center of the plate; top with a grouper filet and finish with the shallot vinaigrette.

Yield: 4 servings

Ocean
1218 20th Street South • Birmingham, Alabama 35205
Phone: 205.933.0999 • oceanbirmingham.com

Herbed Cheese Soufflé with Jumbo Lump Crab and Tomato Concasse

GaBriella's Bistro and Art Gallery

Cheese Soufflé
1 pound cream cheese, softened
1 cup shredded sharp cheddar cheese
1 cup crumbled feta cheese
½ cup chopped green onions
3 ounces chopped green chilies
1 tablespoon minced garlic
3 tablespoons flour
⅓ cup sour cream
3 whole eggs
1 pound jumbo lump crabmeat
1 large heirloom tomato, diced
Prepared cocktail sauce (optional)

Directions:
Preheat an oven to 325°F.

In a standing mixer, mix first 7 ingredients until smooth. Add sour cream and eggs one at a time until mixture is combined. Do not overbeat. Pour mixture into a greased 9-inch springform pan. Tightly wrap side and bottom with foil. Place springform pan in a large shallow pan. Create a water bath by filling up large shallow pan halfway with hot water, taking care not to get any water into the batter.

Bake at 325°F for 1 hour or until center of mixture springs back and does not leave a print when touched.

To serve, top with diced tomatoes and the lump crabmeat. Chef's note: You may also mix the crabmeat with prepared cocktail sauce, if desired.

Yield: 1 soufflé

GaBriella's Bistro and Art Gallery
317 17th Street North • Birmingham, Alabama 35203
Phone: 205.566.2291

Jerk Chicken & Waffles

Roberts Cuisine

6-8 large chicken wings, cleaned,
    washed, and patted dry
Kosher salt
Pure maple syrup for serving

Marinade
1 bunch green onions (scallions), washed and
    chopped
1 large yellow onion
2 or 3 Scotch bonnet peppers, veins and seeds
    removed, peppers chopped
1 tablespoon fresh thyme leaves
1 teaspoon whole cloves
1 head garlic, peeled and chopped
2 tablespoons ground allspice
1 teaspoon coarse ground black pepper
½ tablespoon ground nutmeg
2 tablespoons ground cinnamon
1 tablespoon ground coriander
Juice of 2 limes

Jerk BBQ Sauce
2½ cups Dan's Original (or your favorite
    store-bought BBQ sauce)
2-3 tablespoons jerk marinade
¼ cup pineapple juice
¼ cup orange juice
¼ cup honey

Savory Whole Wheat Waffles
1 cup all-purpose flour
1 cup whole wheat flour
2 tablespoons granulated sugar
4 teaspoons dry mustard
1 teaspoon baking powder
1 teaspoon baking soda
1 teaspoon kosher salt
1 cup buttermilk
1 cup whole milk
½ cup clarified butter
2 eggs
1 tablespoon fresh thyme leaves,
    chopped fine

Directions:

For the Marinade: In a food processor, puree the green onions, yellow onions, Scotch bonnet peppers, thyme, cloves, and garlic. Put in a stainless steel bowl and combine with the allspice, black pepper, nutmeg, cinnamon, coriander, and lime juice. Mix together and refrigerate 4 hours or overnight.

For the Jerk BBQ Sauce: Combine BBQ sauce, jerk marinade, pineapple juice, orange juice, and honey. Set aside.

For the wings: In a stainless steel bowl, liberally season the chicken wings with the kosher salt. Add 1 cup of the jerk marinade, mix well, making sure each piece is thoroughly coated. Add more marinade as necessary. Cover and refrigerate 6-8 hours or overnight.

Roberts Cuisine (Open Sundays Only)
10 6th Avenue South • Birmingham, Alabama 35205
Phone: 205.918.0356 • robertscuisine.com

You can separate the wings into drumette, flat and wing tip buffalo-style, or leave them whole. We recommend leaving them whole while you cook them; it's easier to move them around on the grill, and you have less of a chance of losing a piece between the grill grates.

In a smoker, smoke the wings with pecan or hickory wood for 1½-2 hours at 225°F, until the wings acquire a deep golden color and reach an internal temperature of 170°F. Baste the wings with the Jerk BBQ sauce in the last 5-10 minutes of cooking.

For the Savory Whole Wheat Waffles: Sift the all-purpose flour, whole wheat flour, sugar, dry mustard, baking powder, baking soda, and salt together. In a separate bowl, whisk the milk, buttermilk, butter, and eggs together. Add the wet ingredients to the dry ingredients; add the thyme and whisk together well.

Heat your waffle iron to about medium heat. When it's ready, spoon about 1 cup of the batter into the waffle maker, making sure the batter fully covers the iron (You may need more or less batter depending on your waffle iron.) Close iron and flip; cook for approximately 3 minutes (Your iron may need more or less time.) Yield: 3-4 waffles, depending on how much batter you use.

To serve: Plate waffle with 2 or 3 wings on top and drizzle with pure maple syrup.

Yield: 4 servings

Southern Fried Catfish Over Creole Succotash
The Gardens Café by Kathy G

Southern Fried Catfish
1 boneless (5-7 ounce) catfish fillet
3 ounces all-purpose flour
3 ounces cornmeal
1 teaspoon cayenne pepper
1 teaspoon salt
1 teaspoon pepper
1 teaspoon creole seasoning
2 eggs, lightly beaten
2 tablespoons olive oil

Creole Succotash
2 tablespoons olive oil
½ cup andouille sausage, diced
½ cup red bell pepper, diced
½ cup celery, chopped
1 cup Vidalia onion, diced
1 tablespoon fresh garlic, minced
3 cups fresh baby lima beans
3 cups fresh sweet corn kernels
1 cup fresh tomatoes, diced
½ cup chicken stock
¼ cup fresh parsley
Salt and pepper to taste

Directions:

For the Southern Fried Catfish: Heat the olive oil in a shallow pan/skillet over medium-high heat. In a shallow bowl or pan, mix all of the dry ingredients together. Dip the catfish in the egg mixture, and then place the catfish in the seasoned cornmeal mixture until the fillet is well coated. Pan sear the fillet for 4-6 minutes on each side until it has a golden brown crust. The catfish fillet will be flaky to touch when it is fully cooked.

For the Creole Succotash: Sauté andouille sausage in olive oil; then add bell pepper, celery, and onion. Cook until onion is translucent. Add garlic, being careful not to burn it. Add corn, lima beans, tomatoes, and chicken stock. Cook until tender; finish with fresh parsley, and salt and pepper to taste.

To serve, place the fried catfish over a bed of succotash and garnish with fresh parsley.

Yield: 1 serving

The Gardens Café by Kathy G
2612 Lane Park Road • Mountain Brook, Alabama 35223
Phone: 205.871.1000 • kathyg.com/venues/gardens-cafe

Classic Meat Loaf

5 pounds ground beef
2 medium-sized bell peppers, diced
2 medium-sized onions, diced
½ cup Worcestershire Sauce
1 teaspoon salt
1 tablespoon garlic salt or powder
8-10 ounces milk
2 cups ketchup
¼ cup sugar

Directions:
Place ground beef in a bowl. Add bell pepper and next 5 ingredients. Mix well with hands. Divide mixture among 3 loaf pans. Bake 45 minutes to 1 hour at 350°F.

Remove from oven and drain. Combine ketchup and sugar and stir well to make a glaze. Top loaves evenly with glaze. Return the pan to the oven for 10 minutes to set the glaze. Let rest 5 minutes before slicing.

Yield: 3 loaves

Magic City Grille
2201 3rd Avenue North • Birmingham, Alabama 35203
Phone: 205.251.6500

Nabeel's Moussaka

Nabeel's Café & Market

Appears on the Alabama Department of Tourism's List of "100 Dishes to Eat in Alabama Before You Die"

2½ pounds lean ground beef
3 medium eggplants
1 cup all-purpose flour
1 cup extra virgin olive oil
½ cup butter
1½ large onions, minced
3 cups tomato sauce
½ cup Parmesan cheese
Salt and pepper, to taste
1 cup grated Parmesan cheese

1 tablespoon ground cinnamon
1 tablespoon nutmeg

Béchamel Sauce:
6 tablespoons butter
6 tablespoons all-purpose flour
1 quart milk
1 teaspoon salt
2 eggs

Directions:
Preheat oven to 350° F.

In a large skillet, sauté the onions in olive oil until translucent. Add the beef and brown. Add the tomato sauce, salt, pepper, cinnamon, and mix well. Simmer for about 20-25 minutes. Remove the meat mixture from heat and drain excess oil. Stir in ½ cup of the Parmesan cheese.

To make the Béchamel sauce: In a heavy sauce pan, melt the butter over medium heat. Stir in the flour. Cook, stirring, until the mixture starts bubbling. Remove from heat and with a whisk stir the milk into the flour mixture. Return to medium heat and cook while stirring. Reduce the heat and continue cooking for about 5 minutes, constantly stirring. At this time, the sauce should be very thick. Beat the eggs in a small bowl. Add a spoonful of the Béchamel into the eggs to temper them; then add the egg mixture into the sauce.

To assemble: Sprinkle olive oil on the bottom of a 17x11-inch baking pan. Place a layer of eggplant slices on the bottom. Add a layer of the meat. Repeat 2 more layers, ending with eggplant. Pour the Béchamel sauce over it and spread well to cover the entire baking pan. Sprinkle with nutmeg, cinnamon, and remaining cheese. Bake at 350° F for 45 minutes or until golden brown. Let moussaka cool for 20 minutes and cut into squares.

Yield: 12-15 pieces

Over Easy Famous Oatmeal Pancakes

Over Easy

2 cups flour
2 cups oats (quick oats or 3-minute oats)
¼ cup sugar
1 tablespoon baking powder
2 teaspoons baking soda
2 teaspoons salt
3 cups buttermilk
1 tablespoon vanilla extract
¼ cup vegetable oil
4 eggs

Directions:
Combine all ingredients in a bowl. Whisk until blended. Spray a non-stick spray onto a hot griddle or pan and pour 6-inch wide pancakes. When bubbles form on top of pancakes, flip. Cook until golden brown and delicious.

Top with fresh fruit, powdered sugar, butter, syrup, or any other condiment you like.

Yield: Approximately 12 based on how large you make them.

Over Easy
358 Hollywood Boulevard • Birmingham, Alabama 35209
Phone: 205.639.1910 • overeasybham.com

Panéed Chicken with Mashed Potatoes and Shallot Caper Cream Sauce

Five Bar

2 pounds chicken breasts
3 tablespoons Creole seasoning
    (such as Tony Chachere's), divided
¼ cup olive oil
4 ounces canola oil or other oil for
    frying. You may need to add more
    for each batch

Breading
4 cups all-purpose flour
4 cups Panko breadcrumbs

Mashed Potatoes
5 cloves garlic
10 pounds Yukon Gold potatoes, halved
1½ sticks butter, cut into pieces
1 tablespoon onion powder

3 cups half-and-half
¾ cup sour cream
Salt and pepper to taste

Egg Wash
1 cup eggs, beaten (approximately 5-6 eggs)
1 cup buttermilk

Shallot Caper Cream Sauce
1 cup diced shallots
Olive oil for sauté
½ cup capers
1 cup white wine
½ cup fresh lemon juice
4 sticks butter, cut into pieces
3 ounces heavy cream

Directions:
Preheat oven to 450°F.

Prepare the chicken by trimming the fat from the breasts. Cut each breast in half, keeping each piece of chicken between 4-5 ounces. Place each piece of chicken between two pieces of plastic wrap and pound into ⅛-inch-thick pieces. Toss the chicken with 1 tablespoon Creole seasoning and ¼ cup olive oil. Set aside.

For the Breading: Combine flour and 2 tablespoons Creole seasoning in a large, shallow bowl. Set aside. Put the Panko in a Pyrex large shallow dish or bowl. Set aside.

For the Egg Wash: Put eggs and buttermilk into a bowl large enough to accommodate the chicken and whisk until frothy. Set aside.

For the Mashed Potatoes: Place potatoes in a large saucepan and add water to cover. Bring to a boil. Reduce heat to medium and cook 20 minutes or until potatoes are fully cooked. Remove

Five Bar Birmingham
744 29th Street South • Birmingham, Alabama 35233
Phone: 205.868.3841 • five-bar.com/birmingham

from heat and strain out water. Put potatoes back in pan and add butter and onion powder. Mash well and stir in half-and-half. Put the garlic cloves on a sheet pan and roast at 400°F for 10 minutes or until golden brown. Mince garlic in food processor. Stir the roasted garlic and sour cream into the potatoes and season with salt and pepper to taste. Keep warm.

While the potatoes are cooking, set up a dredge station with the seasoned flour, egg wash, and Panko in that order. Dredge the chicken in the flour, shake off excess. Then, dip chicken into the egg bath. Remove the chicken from the egg and coat with the Panko. Repeat until all of the chicken is coated.

In a large ovenproof skillet, add canola or frying oil. Bring oil to 350°F. Over medium-high heat, place, 3-4 pieces of chicken into the pan and fry to a nice golden brown, then flip and repeat the process on the other side. Once both sides are browned, drain the oil and finish in the oven for 5 minutes or until the chicken is cooked all the way through. Note: The internal temperature of the chicken should be 160°F.

For the Shallot Caper Cream Sauce: Sauté shallots in a large sauté pan in a small amount of olive oil. Season with a pinch of salt and pepper. Once shallots are cooked, deglaze the pan with wine and lemon juice. Let the sauce reduce on low heat until it reaches a syrup-like consistency. Gradually whisk in 4 sticks of butter until it is incorporated. Add the capers and heavy cream. Keep the sauce warm over a double boiler on low heat until ready to serve. (Allowing the sauce to cool will break the sauce, and it will separate.)

Serve the chicken over the potatoes and ladle over 2 ounces of sauce. Garnish with fresh chopped parsley, if desired.

Yield: 4-6 servings

Pork Cutlets Over Chihuahua Cheese Grits with Agave Ancho Chile Maple Sauce

Cantina

Dry Rub Pork Tenderloin
I pork tenderloin, cut into 1-inch cutlets
2 ounces dried chipotle peppers
2 tablespoons olive oil

Chihuahua Cheese Grits
3 cups water with salt and pepper to taste
1 cup quick grits
1 stick butter (½ cup)
1 cup Chihuahua cheese (or substitute with Muenster or medium cheddar cheese)

Agave Ancho Chile Sauce
1 cup maple syrup
1 cup agave syrup
½ cup ground chile peppers

Directions:
For the Dry Rub Pork Tenderloin: Rub dried chipotle peppers into pork tenderloin; slice into 1-inch cutlets. Heat olive oil in skillet and add cutlets; brown on both sides for 3-4 minutes until golden brown. Reduce heat, cover with lid, and simmer for 15-20 minutes.

For the Chihuahua Cheese Grits: Bring water to boil; add grits and butter and cook over medium heat for about 5 minutes. Remove from heat and stir in cheese.

For the Agave Ancho Chile Sauce: Combine all ingredients.

Spoon cheese grits into serving bowl, top with pork cutlet, and drizzle Agave Ancho Chile Sauce over pork before serving.

Yield: 4-6 servings depending on portion size

Cantina
2901 2nd Avenue South Suite #110 • Birmingham, Alabama 35233
Phone: 205.323.6980 • cantinatortillagrill.com

Shrimp and Blue Grits with Bacon Vinaigrette

Little Savannah · Chef/Owners Clif & Maureen Holt

Bacon Vinaigrette
½ pound diced bacon
1 shallot, diced
½ cup sherry vinegar
2 teaspoons light brown sugar
¾ teaspoon Dijon mustard

Blue Grits
3½ cups cold bottled water
1 teaspoon kosher salt
1 cup uncooked organic stone-ground,
    blue corn grits
¼ cup freshly grated Parmesan cheese
2 tablespoons heavy whipping cream
Dash of Tabasco sauce
Additional kosher salt to taste

Shrimp
¼ cup extra-virgin olive oil, divided
½ (8-ounce) package fresh mushrooms,
    quartered
32 large raw shrimp (about 1¾ pounds), peeled
    and deveined, but leave tails on
1 garlic clove, crushed
1 cup white wine
Fresh thyme leaves (about 1 tablespoon)
Fresh minced parsley (about 1 tablespoon)
Reserved cooked bacon (from vinaigrette)
1 cup Bacon Vinaigrette

Directions:

For the Bacon Vinaigrette: Cook bacon in a sauté pan or large skillet over medium heat 8-10 minutes or until browned and crisp. Remove bacon, reserving about ⅓ cup drippings; keep drippings warm. Combine shallot, sherry vinegar, brown sugar, and Dijon mustard; let stand 15 minutes. Whisk drippings into vinegar mixture; keep vinaigrette warm until ready to use. Yield: About 1 cup.

For the Blue Grits: Bring water and 1 teaspoon kosher salt to a boil in medium, heavy saucepan; vigorously whisk in grits. Return to a boil; reduce heat to low and simmer – uncovered – 20 minutes or until thick, stirring every few minutes. Remove from heat; add Parmesan cheese, cream, Tabasco sauce, and additional kosher salt to taste (about 1 teaspoon). Cover and keep warm.

For the Shrimp: While grits are cooking, heat 2 tablespoons oil in large sauté pan or skillet over medium-high heat; add mushrooms, and cook about 5 minutes or until tender. Remove pan and set aside. Using another pan, add remaining 2 tablespoons oil and heat; add shrimp and sauté 1 minute. Add garlic, wine, and kosher salt to taste (about 1 tablespoon). Cook 2-3 more minutes or until shrimp are almost done, stirring occasionally. Add mushrooms, thyme and

Little Savannah
3811 Clairmont Avenue • Birmingham, Alabama 35222
Phone: 205.591.1119 • littlesavannah.com

parsley to shrimp mixture, and cook, stirring constantly, just until shrimp are done. Using a slotted spoon, spoon shrimp mixture over hot grits. Sprinkle bacon and drizzle 1-2 tablespoons bacon vinaigrette over top of each serving. Serve immediately.

Yield: 4 servings

Soy-Marinated Flank Steak with Lemon Relish

Galley & Garden · Chef James Boyce

¾ cup soy sauce
1 clove chopped garlic
1 teaspoon chopped ginger
1 tablespoon chopped mint
1 lemon, zest and juice
1 teaspoon cayenne pepper
1 teaspoon honey
2 pounds flank steak

Lemon Relish
1 large tomato, chopped
2 lemons, zest of one and juice of both
¼ cup olive oil
¼ cup olives, chopped
¼ cup cornichons, chopped
1 tablespoon capers, crushed
1 tablespoon parsley, chopped
Salt and freshly ground pepper to taste

Directions:

Combine first 7 ingredients (soy sauce through honey) and pour over flank steak. Cover and marinate in refrigerator 2 hours.

To prepare Lemon Relish: Combine tomato, lemon juice and zest, and next 7 ingredients. Stir well. Cover and chill.

Heat grill to medium-high heat. Remove flank steak from marinade and discard marinade. Place steak on grill. Sear 5 minutes on the first side and 3 minutes on the other. Remove steak from grill and allow to rest.

To serve, thinly slice flank steak against the grain and present with lemon relish. Serve with warm slices of rustic bread.

Yield: 8 servings

Galley & Garden
2220 Highland Avenue South • Birmingham, Alabama 35205
Phone: 205.939.5551 • chefjamesboyce.com

Stuffed Baby Bells with Romesco Salsa

Chez Lulu/Continental Bakery · Carole Griffin

Romesco Salsa

1 red bell pepper, roasted, seeded, and peeled

1½ slices Continental Bakery Wild Yeast Sourdough bread, fried

2 medium tomatoes (a little more than ¼ pound)

1 head roasted garlic

⅓ cup sliced, toasted almonds

⅓ teaspoon red pepper flakes

2 teaspoons parsley, chopped

⅓ teaspoon paprika

3 tablespoons sherry vinegar

6 tablespoons extra-virgin olive oil, plus a bit more

Salt and pepper to taste

Rice Filling

1 cup rice (prepare according to instructions)

½ cup diced onion

10 ounces cooked garbanzo beans

10 ounces cooked baby lima beans or blanched fava beans

Remaining ¾ head roasted garlic, removed from skin

2 tablespoons chopped Italian parsley

10 ounces tomatoes (peeled, seeded, roughly chopped)

2 ounces grated manchego cheese

Salt and pepper to taste

16-20 small Italian style peppers

½ cup grated manchego cheese, reserve

Directions:

Preheat oven to 400°F.

To roast the pepper: Place the whole red pepper on baking sheet. No oil is necessary. Roast in a very hot oven (400°F) until charred slightly, turning once or twice. Place in a bowl and cover for about 30 minutes, until cool. Working over a bowl to collect any juices, pinch the skins to loosen them from the core to pull them off. Discard the core and slip off the clinging seeds with your fingers. Pass all the juices through a small sieve to remove the seeds. Pour juice over the peppers. Set aside.

Fry bread in a little olive oil until nicely browned and crisp. Set aside.

Roast tomatoes and garlic: In a 400°F oven, place tomatoes and garlic, drizzled with a little of the olive oil. Roast until well caramelized but not burnt, as much as 45 minutes. When cool, peel tomatoes, and squeeze garlic from papery skin, discarding the skin. Use ¼ of the garlic to puree and reserve ¾ of the head for later.

Chez Lulu/Continental Bakery
1911 Cahaba Road • Birmingham, Alabama 35223
Phone: 205.870.7011 • chezlulu.us

To make the Romesco Salsa: When cool, grind bread, nuts, garlic, and red pepper flakes to a smooth paste. This may be done in a mortar and pestle or in a food processor. Add tomatoes to get puree underway. Then add everything else but vinegar and oil, including juices from roasted pepper, and process until fairly smooth, leaving some texture. Gradually add olive oil in a stream. Add vinegar and mix to blend. Season with salt and pepper.

For the Rice Filling: Spread rice in a large flat pan. Add onions, beans, and garlic. When cooled, add parsley, tomatoes, cheese, and salt and pepper, and toss lightly.

Prepare the peppers: Cut tops off the Italian peppers and clean out seeds. Add peppers to salted boiling water for less than 1½ minutes, just until softened. Remove peppers and cool in ice bath. Fill peppers to rim with rice stuffing. Place in roasting pan, cover tightly with aluminum foil, and bake at 350°F for about 45 minutes, until peppers are soft.

Remove from oven, and sprinkle with reserved ½ cup of grated manchego cheese. Place back in oven, or under broiler, until cheese is melted. Garnish with several spoonfuls of Romesco Salsa and serve.

Yield: 6-8 servings

Pepé Le Toast (Stuffed French Toast)

Over Easy

Blueberry Compote
1 pint fresh blueberries
¼ cup sugar
3 tablespoons honey
2 tablespoons lemon juice
1 teaspoon cinnamon
¼ cup water

Sweetened Cream Cheese Filling
16 ounces cream cheese, softened
1½ cups powdered sugar
1 tablespoon vanilla
2 teaspoons cinnamon
1 tablespoon lemon juice

Egg Wash
7 eggs
½ cup milk
1 tablespoon vanilla
1 teaspoon cinnamon

Homemade Whipped Cream
1 cup heavy whipping cream
2 tablespoons confectioners' sugar
1 teaspoon vanilla extract

Sourdough bread of your choice, sliced thick

Directions:

In medium pot, bring all ingredients for the compote to a boil, reduce heat, and simmer for 30 minutes or until mixture begins to thicken. Remove from heat, but keep warm. Meanwhile, blend ingredients for the filling together in a bowl. Set aside.

Prepare Egg Wash: Soak the bread for 2-3 minutes per side.

Make the Homemade Whipped Cream: Put your mixer bowl into the freezer for a few minutes to chill. Add the heavy cream, confectioners' sugar, and vanilla to the bowl. Beat until stiff peaks form.

Heat the pan or griddle. If necessary, spray with non-stick spray or melt some butter to prevent the toast from sticking. Put slices of bread onto the griddle until brown, and bread begins to puff. Flip and repeat on the other side. Remove to plate or pan in a warm oven while you finish the remaining slices.

To assemble: Put a generous amount of the filling between 2½ pieces of the warm French toast. Top with warm compote and the fresh whipped cream. Garnish with blueberries, chocolate shavings, dust with confectioners' sugar, or your favorite toppings.

Yield: 6-8 servings

Over Easy
358 Hollywood Boulevard • Birmingham, Alabama 35209
Phone: 205.639.1910 • overeasybham.com

The Lakeview Pizza
Slice Pizza & Brew

Dough Recipe
2 cups bread flour
½ teaspoon instant yeast
1 teaspoon kosher salt
⅛ teaspoon dried Italian seasoning
1½ teaspoons honey
1 cup water, room temperature
2 tablespoons extra-virgin olive oil
Salt and freshly ground black pepper

Directions:
Divide 4 teaspoons finely chopped garlic (about 5 garlic cloves). In the bowl of a standing mixer fitted with a dough hook, mix together the flour, yeast, salt, and Italian spice blend. In a small bowl, whisk the honey into the water and, with the mixer running, pour the water-honey mixture into the dry ingredients. Scrape down the sides and mix on medium speed for 10 minutes until the dough sticks only to the bottom of the bowl. Cover the bowl with plastic wrap and set aside in a warm place for 1 hour.

Cut the dough into two balls, wrap each loosely with plastic wrap, and refrigerate for 4 hours.

Remove the dough balls from the refrigerator and stretch them into two 10-inch-long rectangles, about ½-inch thick. Rub each portion of dough with a tablespoon of olive oil and season with salt and pepper. Spread 2 teaspoons of garlic evenly over each portion of dough.

Pizza Recipe
Braised beef short ribs (homemade, purchased, or you may substitute other beef)
1 cup caramelized onions
1 cup roasted tomatoes
1 cup Asiago cheese
½ cup red onions
Horseradish Sauce
Arugula for garnish

Slice Pizza & Brew
725 29th Street South • Birmingham, Alabama 35233
Phone: 205.715.9300 • slicebirmingham.com

Caramelized Onions
1 medium yellow onion, sliced into thin half-rings
1 teaspoon olive oil
½ tablespoon butter
Pinch of salt and pepper
1-2 tablespoons liquid to deglaze: water, broth, wine, or balsamic vinegar

Roasted Tomatoes
5-6 Roma tomatoes
2 tablespoons olive oil
2 tablespoons fresh thyme or rosemary, chopped
Salt and pepper

Horseradish Sauce
½ cup sour cream
1 tablespoon cream cheese, softened
1 tablespoon prepared horseradish (find in the seafood department)
1 teaspoon fresh lemon juice
Salt and pepper, to taste

Directions:

To make the Caramelized Onions: Slice a medium yellow onion into thin half-rings. Heat 1 teaspoon olive oil and a small pat of butter in a sauté pan over medium-high heat. Once it is hot, add the onions, salt, and pepper. Stir to coat evenly. Sauté until the onions have softened. Reduce heat and continue cooking over medium-low heat, occasionally scraping up the bits that are forming on the bottom of the pan. As the onions begin to brown, they will begin to stick to the pan. At this point, deglaze the pan with a bit of water, broth, wine, or balsamic vinegar. Continue this process until the onions reach the color and doneness you desire.

To make the Roasted Tomatoes: Preheat the oven to 350°F. Slice the tomatoes in half, right through the middle. Remove the stem on the top. You can first peel the tomatoes, but you don't have to; the peel will slip off after roasting. Pour 1 tablespoon of the olive oil onto your roasting pan. Put tomatoes on the pan, skin side down. Salt and pepper the flesh side of the tomato. Sprinkle with the herbs. Bake at 350°F for 1 hour. Remove and let cool. Remove the peeling and discard. Rough chop the tomatoes into large pieces.

To make the Horseradish Sauce: Mix all ingredients together. Chill.

To build the Pizza: Preheat the oven to 500°F, prior to building your pizza. If you're using a pizza stone, place it in the oven while oven is preheating.

Build pizza by placing braised beef short ribs, caramelized onions, roasted tomatoes, and red onions onto the crust. Top liberally with the Asiago cheese.

continued on next page

Cook on the highest oven temperature for 20 minutes until crust is done and the cheese is melted and browned. Remove and top with arugula and the horseradish sauce. Slice and serve.

Yield: 1 pizza

Desserts

Ted's Famous Baklava

Ted's Restaurant

1 pound Phyllo pastry dough (find in the freezer section of the store)
¾ cup unsalted butter, melted
2 cups walnuts, chopped
1 cup almonds, chopped
¼ cup granulated sugar
2 teaspoons ground cinnamon
⅛ teaspoon ground cloves
2 cups simple syrup

Simple syrup
2 cups granulated sugar
2 cups water
2 tablespoons honey, optional

Directions:
Preheat oven to 325°F.

Handle the Phyllo carefully; keep the unused dough covered with a damp towel. Butter bottom and sides of a 13x9x2-inch oven dish. One at a time, add 9 sheets of Phyllo pastry into the prepared dish, brushing each with melted butter before adding the next sheet.

Mix nuts, sugar, and spices together and spread half of this mixture over the Phyllo.

Top with another 2 sheets of Phyllo, brushing each sheet with butter before adding the next one.

Spread the remaining nut mixture on top and finish with remaining Phyllo, brushing each sheet with butter before adding the next sheet.

Trim the edges and brush the top with butter. Score through the top layers of Phyllo with a knife to create diamond shapes. Sprinkle lightly with water to prevent top layers curling upwards.

Bake on a lower shelf for 30 minutes. Move up one shelf and cook for 30 more minutes. Cover with greased brown paper or tin foil if the top browns too quickly; the Phyllo dough must cook thoroughly.

Ted's Restaurant
328 12th Street South • Birmingham, Alabama 35233
Phone: 205.324.2911 • tedsbirmingham.com

When the Baklava goes in the oven, make the syrup. Boil water and sugar for 10 minutes. Reduce heat and simmer until syrup coats a spoon. Strain.

Spoon the strained syrup over the hot Baklava. Let rest for several hours before cutting into serving portions.

Yield: 30 pieces

Brown Sugar Pound Cake with Bourbon Caramel Glaze

Dreamcakes Bakery & Food Truck

3 cups all-purpose flour (such as White Lily)
½ teaspoon baking powder
¼ teaspoon salt
1 cup whipping cream
1 teaspoon pure vanilla extract
1½ cups butter, softened (3 sticks)
1 (16-ounce) package dark brown sugar
½ cup granulated sugar
5 eggs, room temperature
Bourbon Caramel Glaze
Crumbled bacon (optional)

Bourbon Caramel Glaze
1 cup firmly packed dark brown sugar
1 stick butter
¼ cup evaporated milk
1½ cups powdered sugar
⅛ teaspoon salt
1-2 tablespoons good quality bourbon

Directions:
Preheat oven to 325°F.

Sift together in a medium bowl, flour, baking powder and salt; set aside.

Combine cream and vanilla extract.

Place butter in bowl of electric stand mixer and beat at medium speed until creamy, about 1 minute. Add both sugars and beat on medium-high speed until creamy. Scrape sides with a spatula. Add eggs one at time, beating well after each addition; beat mixture 2 minutes on medium-high speed until light and fluffy. Add ½ flour mixture alternately with ½ of cream mixture; beating on low speed, add remaining flour and cream and mix on low speed just until combined-beginning and ending with flour.

Grease and flour a 10-inch tube pan. Pour batter into prepared pan. Bake at 325°F for 1 hour and 10 minutes (baking times will vary depending on your oven) or until golden brown at edges and a long wooden pick inserted in center comes out clean. Let cool in pan on wire rack for 20 minutes. Remove from pan and cool completely.

For the Bourbon Caramel Glaze: Combine first 3 ingredients in a medium saucepan. Bring to a boil over medium heat, whisking constantly; boil 1 minute. Remove from heat and whisk in

Dreamcakes Bakery & Food Truck
960 Oxmoor Road • Homewood, Alabama 35209
Phone: 205.871.9377 • dreamcakes-bakery.com

powdered sugar and salt until smooth. Stir in bourbon. Whisk gently until mixture is cool and slightly thickened.

Drizzle cooled cake generously and evenly with Bourbon Caramel Glaze; garnish with crumbled bacon if desired.

Yield: 1 cake

Traditional Carrot Cake Cupcakes
Who Doesn't Like Cake Bakery

2 cups all-purpose flour
2 teaspoons baking soda
½ teaspoon salt
2½ teaspoons cinnamon
3 large eggs
2 cups sugar
¾ cup vegetable oil
¾ cup buttermilk
1 tablespoon vanilla extract
2½ cups grated carrots
1 (8-ounce) can of crushed pineapple, drained

1 cup coconut
1 cup walnuts, plus extra for the sides of the cake if you desire

Cream Cheese Frosting
8 ounces unsalted butter, room temperature
16 ounces cream cheese, softened
2 pounds confectioners' sugar
2 tablespoons vanilla extract

Directions:

Preheat the oven to 350°F. Grease and flour 3 (8-inch) round cake pans. You may also spray the pans with Baker's Joy if you prefer. Set aside. For cupcakes, line a cupcake tin with paper cups.

Combine flour, baking soda, salt, and cinnamon in a bowl and set aside. Combine eggs, sugar, vegetable oil, buttermilk, and vanilla in a mixer bowl fitted with a whisk attachment and beat at low speed until combined. Add flour mixture to egg mixture and continue to mix at low speed while gathering remaining ingredients. Add carrots, pineapple, coconut, and walnuts to mixture and mix at low speed until well combined.

Pour batter equally among the 3 prepared cake pans or divide equally among cupcake tins. Bake at 350°F for approximately 20-25 minutes or until done for cake or cupcakes. Allow to cool for 10 minutes in the pan, and then remove from pan onto cooling racks. Cool completely before frosting.

For the Cream Cheese Frosting: Beat butter and cream cheese at high speed of an electric mixer until well combined. Turn mixer to low and add vanilla and confectioners' sugar, a few cups at a time, and continue to beat at low speed until well combined. Turn mixer back to high to beat out any lumps and smooth the frosting.

Who Doesn't Like Cake Bakery
2466 Old Springville Road • Birmingham, Alabama 35215
Phone: 205.856.5777 • whodoesntlikecake.com

To assemble cake: Frost cooled cake layers with Cream Cheese Frosting. First, level the cakes, if necessary. Brush away any crumbs. Put the first layer down and spread icing around the top to the sides of the cake. Repeat with the second layer. Add the third layer. Frost the cake sides and top until smooth. If desired, pipe rosettes around the top border of the cake, using a star tip. Gently press crushed toasted walnuts around the sides of the cake and finish with a sprinkle of walnuts and cinnamon on top of the rosettes. To frost cupcakes, put frosting in Ziploc bag, seal bag, and cut off a bag corner. Pipe frosting atop cupcake. Sprinkle cinnamon and nuts.

Yield: 1 (3-layer) 8-inch cake or 20 cupcakes

Classic Banana Pudding

Fife's Restaurant

1½ cups sugar
Dash of salt
⅔ cup cornstarch
8 cups milk (use any milk)
2 teaspoons vanilla
6 ripe sliced bananas
½ box vanilla wafers

Meringue
10 egg whites
10 tablespoons sugar

Directions:
Preheat oven to 325°F.

Mix cornstarch, salt, and sugar together; blend until smooth with 4 cups milk to make cornstarch mixture. Pour remaining 4 cups of milk into a large pot; add the cornstarch mixture.

Cook over medium heat, stirring constantly, until mixture boils and thickens.

Remove from heat; stir in 2 teaspoons vanilla. Cool for about 10 minutes, stirring occasionally.

Place row of vanilla wafers in large pan. Place row of sliced bananas on top of vanilla wafers. Pour warmed (not hot or wafers will melt) pudding over bananas and wafers until covered. Repeat layers until the top of the pan is reached, ending with a pudding layer.

To make the Meringue: Beat egg whites until foamy. Add sugar slowly until stiff peaks form. With large spoon spread meringue onto top of pudding. Dip spoon onto meringue to make peaks.

Bake at 325°F for 12-16 minutes until nicely browned. Check every minute after 8 minutes.

Yield: 12 servings depending on portion size

Fife's Restaurant
2321 4th Avenue North • Birmingham, Alabama 35203
Phone: 205.254.9167

Peach Cobbler
Fife's Restaurant

½ cup butter
1 (16-ounce) can sliced peaches
1 cup all-purpose flour
1 cup plus 2 tablespoons sugar, divided
¼ teaspoon cinnamon
⅛ teaspoon nutmeg
1 cup milk (whole or 2%)

Directions:
Preheat oven to 325°F.

Melt butter in a saucepan and then pour into an 8x8-inch baking dish to cover bottom.

Add peaches (with syrup) and 2 tablespoons of sugar to saucepan; bring to a boil. Remove from the heat and set aside.

Mix flour, 1 cup of sugar, cinnamon, and nutmeg in a bowl. Stir in milk just until mixture is moistened. Pour half into baking dish over butter.

Pour peach slices and most of the syrup over batter. Spoon remaining batter over slices.

Bake 50-55 minutes until top is golden brown. Cool about 10 minutes and serve.

Yield: 8-10 servings based on portion size

Fife's Restaurant
2321 4th Avenue North • Birmingham, Alabama 35203
Phone: 205.254.9167

Peanut Butter Tofu Pie
The Bottletree

2 packages silken tofu (comes in 12-ounce packages, available at most grocery stores)
1 (16-ounce) jar creamy peanut butter
1 cup confectioners' sugar
4 tablespoons vanilla extract
Pinch of nutmeg
2 graham cracker crusts
Whipped cream
Chocolate syrup

Directions:
Combine the tofu, peanut butter, confectioners' sugar, vanilla and nutmeg in food processor and process until smooth. Spoon evenly into the pie crusts. Cover and refrigerate or freeze for 2 hours before serving. Serve with whipped cream and drizzle chocolate syrup on top.

You can also add chocolate syrup or chocolate malted Ovaltine to the pie filling mixture to your taste to make it even better.

Yield: 1 pie

The Bottletree
3719 3rd Avenue South • Birmingham, Alabama 35222
Phone: 205.533.6288 • thebottletree.com

The Bright Star's Famous Pineapple Cream Cheese Pie

The Bright Star

James Beard Foundation Award Winner

1 (9-inch) deep-dish frozen pie shell, thawed
1 cup cool water
¼ cup cornstarch
2 (8-ounce) cans crushed pineapple in juice
1¼ cups plus 2 tablespoons sugar, divided
1 (8-ounce) package cream cheese, softened

¼ cup all-purpose flour
2 teaspoons vanilla extract
1 egg
⅛ teaspoon yellow food coloring
⅓ cup chopped almonds

Directions:
Preparation: 30 minutes Bake: 30 minutes Cool: 1 hour

Bake pie shell according to package directions until lightly brown. Remove from the oven and let cool.

Then preheat oven to 325°F.

In a small bowl, combine water and cornstarch, stirring until smooth; set aside. In a small saucepan, combine pineapple and ¾ cup sugar. Bring to boil over medium-high heat on stovetop, stirring occasionally. Reduce heat to medium. Stir in cornstarch mixture and bring to a boil, stirring constantly for approximately 5 minutes. Remove from the heat and let stand for 15 minutes.

In a mixing bowl, beat cream cheese, remaining ½ cup sugar plus 2 tablespoons sugar, and flour at medium speed with an electric mixer until creamy. Add vanilla, egg, and yellow food coloring, stirring until smooth.

Add pineapple mixture to cream cheese mixture and mix until combined. Pour mixture into the cooled pie shell. Top with almonds.

Bake for 30 minutes or until a tester inserted near the center comes out clean. Allow to cool on a wire rack for 1 hour before serving. Serve warm or chilled.

Yield: 1 (9-inch) deep dish pie

The Bright Star
304 19th Street North • Bessemer, Alabama 35020
Phone: 205.424.9444 • thebrightstar.com

Gia's Birthday Cake: Pistachio Cake with Honey Marscarpone Mousse and Honey Swiss Buttercream

Gia's Cakes

Every year on Gia's birthday, we get creative in the kitchen and test new flavor combinations. This cake can be made 1-day ahead to ensure best flavor and freshness.

Pistachio Cake

1½ cups cake flour
2¼ teaspoons baking powder
1 teaspoon salt
1 cup light brown sugar
¾ cup unsalted butter
1 (11-ounce) can pistachio paste
7 large eggs
1 tablespoon vanilla extract
2 teaspoons pistachio extract (optional)
2 cups toasted, chopped pistachio nuts for garnish, optional

Directions:

Preheat oven to 350°F for standard oven or 325°F for convection oven.

Sift the dry ingredients into a small bowl and set aside.

Butter and place parchment paper rounds into 3 (8-inch) round cake pans with 1½ inch high sides. Using a stand mixer, cream butter and sugar until light and fluffy. Beat in pistachio paste, gradually scraping down the sides between mixing. Beat until smooth. Gradually add the eggs 2 at a time, making sure they are well incorporated into the batter. Scrape down the sides between additions. Beat in extracts. Using a rubber spatula, fold in the dry ingredients. Divide batter evenly among the pans. Bake cakes until a wooden pick inserted in center comes out clean (about 15 minutes for convection and 20 minutes for standard).

Honey Swiss Buttercream
2 cups egg whites (about 14-16 eggs) (save 7 yolks for mousse)
3¼ cups granulated sugar
2 pounds unsalted butter, room temperature
¼ cup honey
1 tablespoon vanilla

Directions:
Whisk the egg whites and sugar in a bowl over a double boiler. (If you have a heatproof mixer bowl, you can use this over the double boiler.) Whisk periodically to keep whites from cooking. When the mixture reaches 145°F, pour into a mixer and whip on medium-high until soft peaks form. Bring the mixer down to medium-low to allow the mixture to cool. Add butter, small chunks at a time. Bring mixer up to medium-high and whisk until fully incorporated. Add honey and vanilla.

Honey-Mascarpone Mousse Filling
1 cup heavy cream
⅔ cup granulated sugar
7 large egg yolks
1 (16-ounce) container mascarpone, room temperature
¼ cup honey
1 tablespoon vanilla
¼ teaspoon cinnamon
2 gelatin sheets

In a mixer, whisk the heavy cream until soft peaks form. Set aside in the refrigerator until ready to use. Combine the sugar with ¼ cup water and cook in a heavy saucepan until 238-240°F, (soft-ball stage).

Whisk the yolks in a mixer until pale yellow. Carefully pour sugar down the side of the bowl into the yolks, making sure to avoid any sugar hitting whisk. Add honey, vanilla, and cinnamon. Whisk until cooled and volume increases.

While yolk mixture is cooling, soften the gelatin in ice water for 1 minute. Squeeze out excess water and melt down to a liquid over the double boiler used for the meringue. Add this to the yolk mixture while whipping.

Place mascarpone in a bowl and stir to loosen it up. Take a large spoonful of the yolk mixture and stir into the mascarpone. Gradually add this in yolk mixture in three additions, gently folding and well incorporating. Gently fold in the whipping cream in three additions. Mousse can be covered in plastic wrap and set aside for about 1 hour before use.

continued on next page

To assemble: Brush off the cake layers to remove any crumbs. Put a layer of the mousse between each layer of cake. Frost the exterior top and sides of the cake with the buttercream.

To garnish: If you desire, you may add toasted and chopped pistachio nuts to the exterior as indicated in the photo. Put 2 cups pistachio nuts in a food processor and chop. Leave some texture; do not chop too fine. Pour the nuts out onto a sheet pan and toast in the oven at 400°F - just until you can smell them. Watch carefully; nuts burn quickly. Allow the nuts to cool completely. Once cool, carefully press the nuts into the sides of the cake. Leave the top unadorned, creating a swirl pattern with the buttercream.

Yield: 1 (8-inch) layer cake can serve 12 or more depending on portion size.

Ashley Mac's Red Velvet Cake

Ashley Mac's

Cake

1½ cups sugar
1½ cups vegetable oil
2 large eggs
3 (1-ounce) containers red gel icing color, such as Wilton (You can find it at Hobby Lobby,
    Michael's, and other stores where baking supplies are sold.)
1 teaspoon vanilla extract
2½ cups all-purpose flour
2 tablespoons natural unsweetened cocoa powder
1 teaspoon salt
1 cup whole buttermilk
2 teaspoons distilled white vinegar
1½ teaspoons baking soda
1 recipe Cream Cheese Frosting

Cream Cheese Frosting

(8-ounce) package cream cheese, softened
1 cup unsalted butter, softened
3 cups confectioners' sugar
2 teaspoons vanilla extract

Directions:

Preheat oven to 350°F.

Spray 2 or 3 (9-inch) round cake pans with non-stick baking spray with flour like Baker's Joy.
Line with parchment paper, and spray again. Set aside.

In a large bowl, combine sugar and oil, beating at medium speed with an electric mixer until
well blended. Scrape down sides of bowl. Add eggs, beating on low speed. Add gel icing color
and vanilla extract, beating until well blended.

In another bowl, sift together the flour, cocoa, and salt. Add to oil mixture in 3 batches,
alternately with buttermilk, beginning and ending with flour mixture.

Ashley Mac's
Cahaba Heights • 3147 Green Valley Road • Cahaba Heights, Alabama 35243
Inverness • 5299 Valleydale Road • Birmingham, Alabama 35242
Phone: 205.822.4142 • ashleymacs.com

In a small bowl, combine vinegar and baking soda, stirring to blend. Immediately add mixture to cake batter, beating at low speed to combine. (Caution: Do not combine vinegar and baking soda until just before you add to batter.) Divide batter evenly among prepared pans.

Bake approximately 25 minutes or until a wooden pick inserted in the center comes out clean. Let cool in pans for 10 minutes. Remove from pans, and let cool completely on a wire rack.

For the Cream Cheese Frosting: In a large bowl, beat cream cheese at medium speed with an electric mixer until smooth. Add butter, and beat until smooth. Slowly add confectioners' sugar. Stir in vanilla. Yield: approximately 3 cups

Spread Cream Cheese Frosting between layers and on top and sides of cake.

Yield: 1 (9-inch) 2 or 3 layer cake

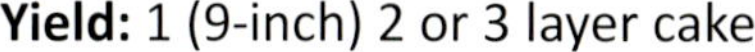

Tahitan Vanilla Créme Brulée

Vino

1 quart heavy cream
1 quart half-and-half
5 vanilla beans
1 cup granulated sugar
16 egg yolks
2 eggs

Directions:
Preheat oven to 350°F. Place 12 small ramekins in a 2-3 inch roasting pan to use for a water bath.

Split the vanilla beans lengthwise, taking care not to cut all the way through. Using your knife, remove the seeds inside. Add the seeds and the pods to a saucepan with the cream and half-and-half. Bring to a slow boil, remove from heat, and let steep for 5 minutes. Remove the pods and discard. Cream the sugar, egg yolks, and eggs together in mixing bowl. In a slow steady stream, pour the heated cream and vanilla mixture into the bowl with the sugar and eggs, mixing continuously. Pour even amounts into the ramekins.

To make the water bath: Fill the pan halfway up the sides of the ramekins with hot water, taking care not to get water into the custard. Bake at 350°F for 1 hour and 15 minutes. The middle of each will be wiggly but set. Carefully remove each ramekin from the water bath and refrigerate.

Before serving, sprinkle the top with a teaspoon or so of sugar, then slowly torch the top to a golden brown.

Yield: 12 (6-7 ounce) Créme Brulées

Note: This recipe can be halved to make a smaller quantity, and the custards can be refrigerated 3-4 days. For Chocolate Créme Brulée, add ½ cup grated bittersweet chocolate to the heated cream mixture, making sure the chocolate is melted thoroughly.

Vino
1930 Cahaba Road, English Village • Mountain Brook, Alabama 35223
Phone: 205.870.8404 • vinobirmingham.com

Tawny Port Wine Flan with Valencia Orange
The Gardens Café by Kathy G

Caramelized Sugar Syrup
½ cup granulated sugar
½ cup water

Custard
1½ cups half-and-half
1½ cups heavy cream
¾ cup sugar
2 teaspoons orange zest
2 tablespoons caramelized sugar syrup
3 whole eggs
3 egg yolks
3 tablespoons tawny port wine
Orange supremes and zest for garnish

Directions:
Preheat oven to 350F°.

For the Caramelized Sugar Syrup: Add water and cook down until it is the consistency of maple syrup. Pour the syrup into bottom of 6-ounce ramekins or a baking mold. Tilt the mold/ramekin in all directions to line the bottom with the syrup. Let cool before adding custard.

For the Custard: Bring the half-and-half, heavy cream and orange zest to a simmer in a heavy saucepan. In a bowl, beat the sugar into the eggs and egg yolks with a whisk until frothy. Gradually pour 1 cup of the cream mixture in a thin stream of droplets into yolks to temper them. Add back into saucepan and heat slowly, stirring constantly for 1 minute. Remove from the heat and stir in the tawny port wine. Strain the mixture through a fine-meshed sieve into the caramel-lined molds.

Set the molds in a water bath; use a 13x9-inch baking dish, and pour boiling water half way up on sides taking care not to get water into the molds. Bake on bottom rack of the pre-heated oven, close oven door, and reduce heat to 325°F. Bake for about 30 minutes; test with a knife until it comes clean when it is inserted in the center. Garnish with Valencia Orange peel and Supremes (orange segments).

Yield: 6 (6-ounce) molds/ramekins

The Gardens Café by Kathy G
2612 Lane Park Road • Mountain Brook, Alabama 35223
Phone: 205.871.1000 • kathyg.com/venues/gardens-cafe

People Are Saying...

By Chanda Temple

In author Todd Keith's 2011 *The Insiders' Guide to Birmingham*, thirty-seven of the book's 290 pages are about restaurants in and around Birmingham. The restaurant section is the book's longest chapter.

"I think I got to 30,000 words, and I had to stop writing,'' Keith says. "Birmingham's a medium-sized town but for its size, we have a ridiculously large number of quality, locally-owned restaurants.''

The Birmingham area offers up a large serving of eateries with diverse dishes that have gained local and national attention. From barbecue and breweries to breakfast spots and beyond-the-basics restaurants, Birmingham's food scene is bold and bright.

"Really, we have it all: posh seafood establishments, the kind of authentic Chinese restaurants you'd expect in San Francisco, white table cloth Italian neighborhood eateries, Southern comfort food, innovative sushi joints, great hot dog stands, better-than-Memphis BBQ, farm-to-table restaurants, craft charcuterie, and a thriving food truck scene. Pair that with an ever-increasing number of top-notch local breweries,'' Keith says. "You don't have to travel out of town for world-class, award-winning culinary options. It's all right here in Birmingham.''

Birmingham leaders agree.

"Over the past thirty-five odd years, Birmingham has developed an outstanding restaurant reputation, not just here locally, but all across the country. I'm excited about the fact that . . . [this cookbook has] recipes from some of our most popular restaurants here in the area so that they can be shared with other people, other individuals to understand and know that Birmingham is moving forward in a quality way as it relates to our restaurants,'' says Birmingham Mayor William A. Bell, Sr.

Like Bell, Dudley Reynolds, retired president and COO of Alagasco, applauds the idea of such a cookbook in Birmingham. "It is very gratifying and not surprising to see our culinary community coming together and sharing recipes to support such a great cause. Cooking truly brings us together.''

Adds Bell: "I want to thank all of the chefs who make it possible to have such great food here in Birmingham, Alabama. We look forward to continuing to grow that arena because it helps attract people to come here for conferences and conventions. When people come here and they see the fine quality of life, with the fine food that we have, it makes them want to live here as well.''

Here's what some people have to say about their favorite local restaurants:

Gwen Amamoo, former Birmingham Public Library Board President, on Rib-It-Up, 830 1st Avenue North, Birmingham: "Their food is well seasoned and tastes like my mom and Big Mama's cooking. I like the potato salad and the ribs. My favorite choice is the cracklin' muffins."

Taylor Hicks, 2006 American Idol Winner and Co-Owner of Saw's Juke Joint, 1115 Dunston Avenue, Birmingham: "I promise you that our Saw's Wings are the best in town. I challenge you to find better. You won't!"

Shanta' Owens, a Jefferson County district judge, on Pastry Art Bake Shoppe, 1927 29th Avenue South, Homewood: "The Baby Bites (miniature cake bites) at Pastry Art are absolutely delicious. Whenever I pick up an order for an event, I get an extra one to eat in the car. They are that hard to resist. Red velvet is my favorite.''

Donta Wilson, Group/State President of BB&T, on Sammy's Sandwich Shop, 4921 Messer Airport Highway, Birmingham: "Run to Sammy's Sandwich Shop for perhaps the best burger in Alabama, and the most diverse 'melting pot' lunch experience one can enjoy from business movers and shakers to politicians to construction workers. Great food and great fellowship."

Tracey Morant Adams, senior vice president, small business and community development director at Renasant Bank, on Five, 744 29th Street South, Birmingham: "When guests visit us, we love showcasing trendy eating in the city, which includes having brunch at Five on Sundays and enjoying those incredible apple beignets!"

Eric Welch Guster, Birmingham attorney and legal analyst, on Jim N' Nick's at the Birmingham-Shuttlesworth International Airport: "I enjoy the Jim 'N Nick's barbecue at the airport because it's my last taste of home before flying to New York to be on FOX, MSNBC and CNN. It's hard to find great barbecue in New York, so I grab a little bit of home to go."

Roy Wood, Jr., Los Angeles comedian, on Milo's Hamburgers, various Birmingham locations: "True story. I had been out of Birmingham for about a 1½ years, and I hadn't had Milo's for a year. I was traveling and had a connecting flight through Atlanta. I had a four-hour layover which, with my calculations, was enough time to rent a car, drive to Pell City, Alabama, go to Milo's and be back in Atlanta for my connecting flight. I drove to Pell City, I bought two sandwiches, and I made my flight. I ate one sandwich, and I had the second one on the plane.''

Eric Essix, Birmingham musician, on Cantina Tortilla Grill at Pepper Place, 2901 Second Avenue South, Birmingham: "Cantina is a great place to get quality food in a nice atmosphere with excellent service by a very friendly and attentive staff. My favorite meal is the Tortilla Encrusted Tilapia."

Ebony Steele, Atlanta entertainer, on Surin West, 1918 11th Avenue South, Birmingham: "When I'm in Birmingham, I must have the Pad Prik Chicken from Surin West. From Atlanta to LA, there is no sauce that compares to that of the Pad Prik.''

Rickey Smiley, national comedian and syndicated radio host, on the Original Pancake House, 1931 11th Avenue South, Birmingham: "I love the breakfast steak, and I'm thrilled that I've had the same waitress there for years.''

Eunice Elliott, Birmingham television and radio personality, on Saw's Soul Kitchen, 215 41st Street South, Birmingham: "Very unique menu items bursting with down-home goodness."

Dr. Craig Witherspoon, former Birmingham City Schools Superintendent, on John's City Diner, 112 Richard Arrington Boulevard, Birmingham: "I always enjoy eating at John's. There are plenty of excellent selections, large portions, and great prices. I love their bread pudding."

Sherri Ross on Mia Luna, 728 29th Street South, Birmingham: As founder of the Birmingham Girls Club, a group dedicated to giving back to the community, Ross started inviting members to visit area restaurants once a month to network and discover new foods. She's a Mia Luna fan. "I love the sausage balls . . . and the homemade pepper jelly sauce that comes with it."

Joe Lockett, radio host of the Joe Lockett Show, on Yo' Mama's, 2328 Second Avenue North, Birmingham: "I like the chicken and waffles. Their waffles are fluffy. They melt in your mouth. The chicken, I've never tasted chicken like that. And when you combine them with that homemade syrup, it's like one big explosion of taste in your mouth."

Melva Tate, a career coach, on Wasabi Juan's, 4120 3rd Avenue South, Avondale: "Their creative fusion of Mexican and Asian resulted in the most amazing sushi I've ever eaten. I tried the Destin and the Samurai. They have been added to my must-visit list for clients and friends."

Ann Murphy on Redeaux's Cafe at City Hall, 710 20th Street North, Birmingham : "The food is always fresh and seasoned well. They serve breakfast and lunch, offering something different every day. I love their jambalaya. It's to die for."

Brandan "B-Stuc" Stuckey on Iron City, 513 22nd Street South, Birmingham: "Their wings are second to none. And their burger reminds you of something you'd find at a cookout. There's flavor in every bite. It's a great place to eat and watch the game when they have those types of events."

Rickey White, Jr. on Avondale Brewery, 201 41st Street South, Birmingham: "I love Avondale Brewery. It's like a big family patio. On a Saturday afternoon, with a couple of beers and friends, you'll never go home."

Deon Gordon, director of business growth at REV Birmingham on Babalu Tacos & Tapas, 2808 7th Avenue South, #117, Birmingham: "Great staff. Great service. Some of the freshest ingredients I've ever tasted in their salsa. Outstanding!"

Joseph Baker on BYOB Rocks (Build Your Own Burger), 720 29th Street South, Birmingham: "They have this nice array of different burger options: BBQ style, super spicy . . . Southwest . . . turkey burgers. I enjoyed it. "

Daniel Walters on Mia Luna, 728 29th Street South, Birmingham: "I've had their smoked turkey sandwich with jalapeno aioli. Who would have thought to put jalapeno aioli on a smoked turkey sandwich? It was amazing! If you like spicy, you are going to love the sandwich."

Anne Rast Yoder on Slice Pizza & Brew, 725 29th Street South, Birmingham: "At Slice, the Bajalieh brothers kill it with the White Shadow pie, a perfectly balanced combination of garlic, grilled onion, mushroom, feta and Parmesan (cheeses) finished with truffle oil. Yum!"

Donna Francavilla on Highlands Bar and Grill, 2011 11th Avenue South, Birmingham: "Whenever I dine there, I see and can mingle with interesting people, many of whom play integral rolls in the city. The atmosphere is elegant; the vibe feels positive, vibrant."

Vanessa Culpepper on Café DuPont, 113 20th Street North, Birmingham: "A beautiful, quaint spot. Perfect for special occasions with a diverse dessert menu to satisfy any sweet tooth."

Genesis Player on Giuseppe's Cafe, 925 8th Street South, Birmingham: "Giuseppe's is one of Birmingham's best kept secrets for Italian food. Their pizzas are to 'live' for!"

Demetrius Caldwell on Steel City Pops at the Summit, 329 Summit Boulevard, Birmingham: "Steel City Pops is a must anytime my family and I visit from Huntsville, Alabama. Buttermilk is my mainstay. My wife and 15-year-old daughter prefer the fruity pops. My two-year-old daughter devours the Vanilla Bean."

Kimberly McNair Brock on Shangri-La 4500 Montevallo Road, Birmingham: "My favorite meal, which I've never had a bad one, would be Hunan Shrimp-Stir Fry. The veggies are just the right texture, and the sauce is just perfect for soaking up the yummy rice. I always get their egg rolls as an accompaniment."

Comedienne Joy, the Queen of Clean, on Shark's Fish and Chicken, 254 Green Springs Highway, Birmingham: "The honey barbecue wings and fries are the best at Shark's. Their food is cooked to order and worth the wait."

Birmingham Radio Host Matt Murphy on Bottega Café and Sammy's Sandwich Shop, 4921 Messer Airport Highway, Birmingham: "It is hard to go wrong with the Café Mac and Cheese at Bottega Café. It's creamy and comes with that little crisp from the browned Parmesan cheese on top. It's a decadent treat that will change your idea about what simple pasta and cheese can be. For a hidden gem, try Sammy's Sandwich Shop. They have been around for about fifty years or so. They are an institution. The burger is like one your mom would make."

Karri Bentley on Over Easy, 358 Hollywood Boulevard, Birmingham: "I love the Hash Brown Basket. The restaurant is bright and inviting. The service is great. And the food is so good."

Anne Rast Yoder on Satterfield's, 3161 Cahaba Heights Road, Birmingham: "I once had a pork chop at Satterfield's that was so perfectly wonderful that I have not been able to bring myself to make pork chops at home since. They elevate the mere pork chop to a whole new high."

Paul Rogers on GianMarcos, 721 Broadway Street, Homewood: "If you get me the GianMarcos Penne Alla Vodka recipe, we will be best friends! It's my favorite dish because it's good, it's simple, and versatile. It works with almost any meat - beef, chicken, pork, even seafood."

Williesha C. Morris on Urban Cookhouse, various locations: "I've only been there once, but it made a huge impression on me. I had the Berry Good Salad with berries, tomatoes, spiced pecans, feta, and citrus vinaigrette topped with chicken salad . . . I love the orange rolls, too."

Deidra Perry on El Barrio Restaurante Y Bar, 2211 2nd Avenue North, Birmingham: "El Barrio is my favorite local restaurant, hands down. My favorite dish is the vegetarian quesadilla. I love the bubbly melted cheeses layered with spinach, mushrooms, and fresh corn. This dish never disappoints!"

Willette McKinney Boyd on Jim 'N Nick's, various Birmingham locations: "I love their cheese biscuits, French fries, baked beans, and cole slaw."

Karri Bently on Niki's West, 233 Finley Avenue, Birmingham: "Niki's has been a staple in my family for years. It's where I always go for lunch to celebrate my birthday. Best fried green tomatoes in my opinion."

Yolanda Davis on Green Acres, various Birmingham locations: "Whenever I come home to Birmingham (from Mississippi), I find a way to get three wings "all the way." That's with hot sauce and ketchup. Simple and always good."

Gwendolyn B. Guster Welch on The Harbert Center, 2019 4th Avenue N #100, Birmingham (Catering by Southern Food Services Management, Inc.): "Whenever I'm at the Harbert Center for a meeting or banquet, I can't wait to have one of their homemade desserts. My favorites are the banana pudding and berry cobblers. That pecan pie is high on my list, too."

Niya Pickett Miller on Chop Suey Inn, 813 Green Springs Highway, Homewood: "I love how hot the food stays during my drive home. They pack the cartons out. My favorite dish is the special fried rice, beef, broccoli, and sesame chicken 'with light sauce.' "

Willie Davis on Corry's Restaurant, 1800 24th Street, SW, Birmingham: "I absolutely love their grilled chicken salad because it's seasoned to perfection. The chicken is piled high on top of a bed of fresh lettuce, plump ripe tomatoes, cheese, seasoned boiled eggs, fresh green onions, and Ranch dressing."

Russell Lee on Full Moon Bar-B-Cue, various locations: "Their cole slaw is a vinegary, tangy, and sweet mixture of goodness. It's almost like chow chow or relish that would be good on a barbecue sandwich, a hot dog, or piled on top of your favorite peas or beans."

Toni Pierce on Ocean, 1218 20th Street, South, Birmingham: "Locally owned and operated, they have the best and freshest seafood in town."

Sherri Goodman on GianMarcos, 721 Broadway Street, Homewood: "When my husband and I can sneak away for a date, we love the cozy wine bar behind the restaurant. We know we will get excellent food and service in a comfortable, unpretentious setting."

Darold Mathews on Chris Z's, 2808 University Boulevard; Ted's Restaurant, 328 12th Street South; and Fish Market, 612 22nd Street South, all in Birmingham: "Chris Z's has . . . one of the best BLTs in Birmingham. (Get it on rye.) I love the vegetable selection at Ted's. The spinach, shrimp, and chick pea dish is a must try at the Fish Market!"

Sam Jackson on Highlands Bar and Grill, 2011 11th Avenue South, Birmingham: "The Beef Carpaccio at Highlands is exquisite. It's even better than the original at Harry's Bar in Venice."

Mary Schuchman Hendley on Bettola, 2901 Second Avenue South, Birmingham: "My favorite (pizza) is the Melanzane E Pepperoni - eggplant and roasted peppers. But the dish Funghi Di Bosco - Crimini e portobello mushrooms and truffle oil is a very close second."

Debbie McCune on Davenport's Pizza, 2837 Cahaba Road, Mountain Brook Village: "I have been going to Davenport's since my high school days. I crave their chilled iceberg salad with homemade dressing. It is the best salad in town. The 'chilled' is what makes it great!"

Caroline Sayre on Saw's Soul Kitchen, 215 41st Street South, Birmingham: "My favorite Birmingham bite is the pork and greens plate at Saw's . . . It is everything I crave about barbeque, all loaded up on one plate covered in their sauce. I ate this twice a week while I was pregnant!"

Scott Young on Ocean, 1218 20th Street South, Birmingham: "Without hesitation, I like the Wood-Roasted Lobster Tail at Ocean. I follow that up with the scallops. You cannot get fresher or better seafood in the city."

Jared Lewis on Hot and Hot Fish Club, 2180 11th Court South, Birmingham: "My mom's meatloaf is the best bite in Birmingham, but my favorite dish at a restaurant has to be the Hot and Hot Tomato Salad."

Stacy Clayton on O'Carr's Delicatessen, 2909 18th Street South, Homewood: "Skip the meal and go straight for the cheesecake. I'm not a big fan of desserts but this one is to die for. Creamy and light, it is a piece of heaven."

Jodie Perry on Jinsei Sushi, 1830 29th Avenue South, Homewood: "I don't eat sushi but absolutely love the tuna dish from Jinsei. I could eat it every day. Add the green beans or the edamame. And a freshly made cocktail."

Lynn Walton on Salvatore's Pizza and Pasta, 4673 Highway 280, Inverness: "Salvatore's is our family favorite. Their marinara is the best in town. Salads are so fresh, and they make a house dressing they sell by the bottle. We love it."

Where the Pros Go...
Those in the food business know good food. Here are some of their favorites:

Maureen Holt of Little Savannah on Chen Express, 221 Country Club Park, Mountain Brook: "Our crew likes the 'chicken on a stick' from Chen Express in Crestline for lunch during a busy day. It's a five-spice rubbed chicken thigh that is slow roasted and so good. It's even good at the end of our night!"

John Coon of House of Q BBQ and BBQ Pitmasters on Destination America, about Niki's West, 233 Finley Avenue West, Birmingham and Bottega, 2240 Highland Ave South, Birmingham: "The Trout Almandine at Niki's is an all-time favorite of mine. My wife and I love going to Bottega Café, especially when the weather is nice, so we can sit outside on the patio."

Isabella Alexander, pastry chef at Darlings Sweets Bakery, on Jim n' Nick's, 1908 11th Avenue South, Birmingham and other locations: "As a baker, I always want to try the baked goods when I eat at a restaurant. The Cheese Biscuits at Jim 'n Nick's are my very favorite!"

Jason Burnett, Founding Editor of MyRecipes.com, on Bettola, 2901 2nd Avenue South, Birmingham: "No matter how many times I order Bettola's Calamari Arositi, the first bite always makes me say, 'Life is good!' A simple sugo du pomodoro with red peppers and fresh herbs proves that quality ingredients can make the humblest of foods dazzling."

Chef Chris Vizzina on The Fish Market, 612 22nd Street South, Birmingham and Highlands Bar and Grill, 2011 11th Ave South, Birmingham: "Grilled grouper on a large Greek Salad from The Fish Market reminds me of my trips to Greece. Of course, anything at Highlands is wonderful, but I'm very fond of the Stone Ground Baked Grits with Country Ham, Mushrooms, Thyme, and Parmesan cheese because I was very fortunate to cook them numerous times in Chef Stitt's kitchen."

Chef/Owner Jake Reed of Albany Bistro in Decatur, Alabama on Ollie Irene, 2713 Culver Road, Mountain Brook: "I don't get to Birmingham often enough, but when I do, I head to Ollie Irene in Mountain Brook Village for the boudin balls!"

Chef Wesley True, James Beard Award Semi-Finalist of True Restaurant in Montgomery, Alabama, on Bottega Café, 2240 Highland Ave South, Birmingham: "One of my fondest memories of working as a chef in New York City was the incredible thin crust pizza we'd get after work. Every time I eat that super crispy thin crust pizza at Bottega Café, I'm immediately transported back to that time and the fond memories of New York."

Tailgate Guru and Tony Chachere Tailgate Competition Winner Brad O'Rear on Ragtime Café, 2080 Valleydale Road #4, Hoover: "The filet topped with crabmeat is one of my all-time favorites. It is served with a twice-baked potato and veggies. You have to try this one."

Martie Duncan on Chez Fonfon, Hot and Hot Fish Club, 2180 11th Court South, Birmingham and The Pita Stop, 1106 12th Street South, Birmingham: "I absolutely love Chez Fonfon. I always feel like I've traveled to Paris, and I'm at my favorite bistro. I call Chez Fonfon 'my office.' I have all of my meetings there over a cappuccino and housemade dessert. The Chocolate Pots du Créme or the Lemon Tarts have to be a favorite. Also, the chef's counter at Hot and Hot Fish Club is a great place to eat, watch the chefs at work, and see how a professional kitchen is really done right. And I love the fact that my friend Tena Payne's beautiful Earthborn Pottery lines the counter, too. For family night, we have been going to The Pita Stop for over thirty years, and it is still as good as it ever was. I always get the Chicken Kabob Plate and have never ordered anything else."

Not Hungry?
Here Are Some Things To Do In and Around Birmingham
By Chanda Temple

The heartbeat of Birmingham lies in its people and its places. From its diverse nightlife and dining to its eclectic art and entertainment, Birmingham serves up hearty cuisine, attractions, and culture that keep people coming back for more.

Here's a glimpse of some of the best that the city has to offer:

Relive the glory days of your favorite Alabama sports legends at the **Alabama Sports Hall of Fame**, 2150 Richard Arrington, Jr. Boulevard, where more than 5,000 sports artifacts are housed. Be sure to look for items from Jesse Owens, Hank Aaron, Willie Mays, Joe Louis, and Carl Lewis, five of ESPN's top 15 North American Athletes of the 20th Century.

Watch classic movies and soak up elaborate architecture at the **Alabama Theatre**, 1811 Third Avenue North. Built in the 1920s, this "Showplace of the South" is definitely a "do" in the city.

Alabama Theatre

Go for a wine adventure on three Alabama wineries along the **Alabama Wine Trail**. They include Morgan Creek Vineyards in Harpersville, Alabama; Ozan Vineyard and Winery in Calera, Alabama; and Vizzini Farms Winery in North Calera, Alabama.

See a collection of 19th-century furniture, paintings, and textiles at **Arlington Antebellum Home & Gardens**, 331 Cotton Avenue. It dates to the 1840s.

Feed your need for speed at the **Barber Motorsports Park & Museum**, 6040 Barber Motorsports Parkway. More than 1,200 vintage and modern motorcycles from 17 nations and 125 manufacturers are at the museum. World-class car and motorcycle races are held at its track.

Sixteenth Street Baptist Church

Catch the **Birmingham Barons**, a minor league team that won the Southern League Championship Series in 2013, play ball at Regions Park, 1401 First Avenue South. It is across the street from the award-winning **Railroad Park**, 1600 First Avenue South, where people run, play, and have fun in the sun any day of the week.

Visit the **Birmingham Civil Rights Institute**, **Sixteenth Street Baptist Church**, **Kelly Ingram Park**, the **Fourth Avenue Black Business District**, and the **Alabama Jazz Hall of Fame**, all in or near the 500 block of 16th Street North, for a griping lesson on the city's role in the civil rights movement.

Stop and smell the roses at the **Birmingham Botanical Gardens**, 2612 Lane Park Road, where a wide variety of plants and flowers can be found on its sixty-seven acres.

Experience art from around the globe at the **Birmingham Museum of Art**, 2000 Reverend Abraham Woods, Jr. Boulevard, which has more than 26,000 sculptures, paintings, drawings, and more.

Birmingham Public Library

Read more than a book at the **Birmingham Public Library**, 2100 Park Place, where the options of discovery and learning are endless. There are millions of artifacts, photographs, and resources in the downtown library's archives department, free computer classes, playtime and story time for preschoolers, genealogy classes, book downloads, movies, music, and more. You name it, the Birmingham Public Library and its eighteen locations likely have it. And it's all free.

Visit lions, tigers, and bears at the **Birmingham Zoo**, 2630 Cahaba Road, where more than 900 animals call it home. Check out the male African elephants in the Trails of Africa exhibit or glide through the tree tops of the Jane H. Brock Soaring Safari Zipline Adventure.

Take in a movie, do a science project, and see marine life at the **McWane Science Center**, 200 19th Street North. The center has an IMAX Dome Theater, aquarium, and four floors of interactive exhibits.

Climb the massive sandstone boulders or explore the wildlife at the **Moss Rock Preserve**, 4335 Village Green Circle. Ten miles of trails are on this 350-acre nature preserve, which also has streams and small waterfalls.

Take a hike, sunbathe or ride a bike at **Oak Mountain State Park**, 200 Terrace Drive in Pelham, Alabama. With 9,940 acres that offer 50 miles of hiking, biking, and equestrian trails, it's the state's largest park.

Go nuts over the **Peanut Depot**, 2016 Morris Avenue, where freshly roasted, salted, and Cajun peanuts are sold. They've been in business since 1907.

Enjoy the panoramic views of the city atop **Red Mountain at Vulcan Park and Museum**, 1700 Valley View Drive. Built in 1904, the statue is the world's largest cast-iron statue and is also a nod to the city's industrial history.

Vulcan Statue

Celebrate baseball history at **Rickwood Field**, 1137 Second Avenue West, the former home of the Birmingham Barons and Birmingham Black Barons. Built in 1910, it is known as "America's Oldest Baseball Park." It has seen baseball greats such as Babe Ruth, Ty Cobb, Jackie Robinson, Willie Mays, and Satchel Paige. Movies such as *Cobb* and *42* have been filmed there.

Tee it up at **Robert Trent Jones Golf Trail**, a collection of public golf courses across Alabama. The picturesque courses are challenging, though inviting, for players of all skill levels. Courses in the Birmingham area are located at Oxmoor Valley, 100 SunBelt Parkway, and Ross Bridge, 4000 Grand Avenue.

Be one with nature at **Ruffner Mountain Nature Preserve**, 1214 81st Street South, the third largest urban nature preserve in the United States.

Learn more about Birmingham's humble beginnings as an iron and steel town by visiting **Sloss Furnaces**, 20 – 32nd Street North.

Soar high at the **Southern Museum of Flight**, 4343 73rd Street North, one of the largest aviation museums in the South. The museum has more than 90 aircraft, plus photographs, engines, and artifacts.

Southern Museum of Flight

Beat the heat at the **Splash Adventure Waterpark**, 4599 Alabama Adventure Parkway, which has a wave pool; a nine-story Acapulco Drop; an interactive play area with geysers, pumps, and buckets; inner tube rides; and more.

Eat up, sleep in, or take in the sites at the **Uptown district**, 2221 Richard Arrington, Jr., Boulevard, home to six eateries, one coffee shop, two hotels, and Alabama's largest entertainment and convention complex.

Uptown District Photo Credit: kp studios

Hungry now? The choices of where to eat in Birmingham are plentiful, while the experiences are endless. Don't know where to start? Check out the IN Guide (birminghamal.org/INguide/) for a list of popular restaurants, coffee houses, and bakeries, several of which are included in this cookbook. Love farm-fresh produce, international fare, or unique shopping spots? You can find Birmingham locations for those in the guide, too.

For more information on what's in Birmingham, visit birminghamal.org/about/, which provides the perfect road map to discovering or rediscovering the heart and soul of the city.

Photos courtesy of Alabama Theatre, Birmingham Public Library, Southern Museum of Flight, and Vulcan Park and Museum. Sixteenth Street Baptist Church photo by Chanda Temple.

Contributors

Connie Blalock, *Restaurant Liaison*
Connie Lyle Blalock is the president of The Total Package, a market planning and events coordinating company working with businesses, corporations, and individuals. With more than thirty years of experience including advertising, marketing, consumer education, and culinary arts, in addition to publishing more than ten cookbooks, Connie is also active in the Les Dames Birmingham Chapter, The Birmingham Originals, and the American Culinary Federation Alabama Chapter.

Anne Cain, *Recipe Editor*
Anne Cain is the director of communications for the Southeast Dairy Association. Prior to working with the dairy industry, she was at Southern Progress Corporation for twenty-four years as a cookbook food editor and as the senior food editor at MyRecipes.com.

Moesia (Mo) Davis, *Photographer, Arden Photography*
Mo Davis is an Alabama native and came to Arden Photography in 2012. She fell in love with photography at a young age and has had a camera by her side ever since. Mo has styled hundreds of food photos in her career. She shoots many of Birmingham's social occasions and charity events. Wedding photography is her specialty.

Martie Duncan, *Project Manager*
Party expert and entrepreneur Martie Duncan represented the great state of Alabama and home cooks everywhere as a finalist on seasons eight and ten of the popular competition cooking show, *Food Network Star*. Martie has helped plan everything from big weddings and charity events to casual tailgates and backyard picnics. Her popular website, MartieKnowsParties.com, showcases her easy-to-follow recipes and ideas for affordable entertaining at home. As the party expert for Time Inc.'s MyRecipes.com, her Martie Knows Parties videos are consistently one of the site's most popular features. She's currently at work on her first book and is busy appearing at food events across the country, including appearances with Guy Fieri, Bobby Flay, and other Food Network personalities.

Grace Headman, *Index Writer*
Grace Headman graduated from Samford University in 2012 with a degree in Journalism and Mass Communication. Shortly afterwards, she scored a position at Southern Progress Corporation with MyRecipes.com, doing everything from recipe production to social media and blogging. The highlight of Grace's experience was the opportunity to travel with Martie Duncan during her delicious Alabama Restaurant Week excursion in 2012 and 2013, providing logistical and social media assistance. While Grace has recently moved on from her time at MyRecipes, her love for cooking has only grown. She can't wait to share *Birmingham's Best Bites* with friends and family!

Dr. Joyce Pettis, *Editor*

Dr. Joyce Pettis, formerly a professor of English at North Carolina State University, is a writer and editor in her retirement. She lives in Huntsville, Alabama. This is her first editing venture with a cookbook.

Lisa Mitchell Smith, *Graphic Designer*

Lisa Mitchell Smith has been a graphic artist for fourteen years. She currently works in the Public Relations Department at the Birmingham Public Library. She also does design work for individuals and various organizations throughout the United States. In her spare time, Lisa enjoys spending time with her family.

Chanda Temple, *Writer*

Chanda Temple is a former journalist now working in public relations in Birmingham, Alabama. No matter the person or the project, she's committed to using public relations to help push a story. In her spare time, she enjoys spending time with family, public speaking, and helping students and adults with writing and networking. Chanda has received numerous awards and recognition for her writing and community work. In 2014, Birmingham Magazine selected her as one of the "20 Women Who Make a Difference." In 2013, she received a Distinguished Leadership Award for Excellence in Communications. She blogs at chandatemplewrites.com. *Photo credit: Elle Danielle Photography*

Arden Ward Upton, *Photographer*

Arden Ward Upton shot her first wedding in 1999. Fifteen years later, Arden Photography has grown to house three photographers specializing in celebrations, editorials, and portraits. Food, of course, is always a favorite subject. Her recent collection of equestrian-inspired prints launched to rave reviews and can be seen in her Crestline, Alabama, studio and art galleries around the country. Arden gives time to charity projects in and around Birmingham. She donated all of the beautiful photography for this book.

Chris Vizzina, *Recipe Coordinator*

A graduate of the New England Culinary Institute, Chef Chris Vizzina has worked at many respected establishments - from The Ritz Carlton to the legendary Highlands Bar and Grill. Formally with Campus Dining, Inc. at Samford University, Chef Vizzina embraces some of the principles and values from mentors George Sarris, Frank Stitt, and Danny Lassiter. He believes in buying locally, sustainability practices, and cooking with the seasons. Chef Vizzina works with local schools, churches, and other organizations and shares his love of cooking to live a healthy and full life. Chef Vizzina was one of the first to adopt a school (Homewood High School) many years ago to help get children on the path of making better food choices.

Recipe Index

Cocktails & Drinks

Starters & Sides

Salads, Soup & Sandwiches

The Main Course

Restaurant Index

A

Ashley Mac's: 31, 187

B

Baumhower's: 101
Bellinis: 8, 129
Bettola: 51
Bob Sykes BarB-Q: 120
Bottega: 133
Bottega Café: 135
Bottle & Bone: 106
Brick & Tin: 74

C

Cantina: 154
Carrigan's Pub: 82
Century Restaurant at the Tutwiler Hotel: 128
Chez Fonfon: 43
Chez Lulu/Continental Bakery: 159
Copper Pot Kitchen: 132
Crestwood Café: 70, 96

D

Dixie Fish Company: 54
Dodiyo's: 39
Dreamcakes Bakery & Food Truck: 171
Dreamland Bar-B-Que: 66

E

Eagles Restaurant: 42
El Barrio Restaurant y Bar: 17, 35, 38

F

Fife's Restaurant: 58, 176, 177
Five Bar: 13, 151
FoodBar: 62
Full Moon Bar-B-Que: 47, 124

S

T

V

W

Z

Ingredients Index

A

Almonds

B

Bacon

Bananas

Basil

BBQ

Beans

Beef (See also: Beef, Ground)

Beef, Ground

Bourbon

Blueberries

Brown Sugar

C

Cabbage

Carrots

Catfish